Dance of the Sun Goddess

Pagan Folkways of the Baltic Coast

About the Author

Kenneth Johnson was quite literally born and raised in "Surf City USA" – he grew up in south California during the 1960s. He obtained his B.A. in Comparative Religions at California State University Fullerton and his M.A. in Eastern Studies at St. John's College in Santa Fe, NM.

For some years a staff writer for The Mountain Astrologer, Kenneth also participated in Project Hindsight, a colloquium of astrological scholars dedicated to restoring and interpreting the earliest known texts on horoscopic astrology.

Kenneth has published many books. His best-known works are *Mythic Astrology* (co-authored with Arielle Guttman), a vast reference work on the archetypal symbolism which lies behind all the planets and signs used in astrology (and still in print after 29 years), as well as *Jaguar Wisdom: An Introduction to the Mayan Calendar*—carried through Latin America by gringo travelers for many years now, right next to their Lonely Planet guidebooks. His works have been translated into German, Portuguese, Japanese, Czech, Russian and Bulgarian.

An inveterate world traveler, Kenneth is currently ensconced in a remote Mayan town in the mountains of Guatemala where, after ten years of study, he was initiated into the indigenous Mayan priesthood as an aj q'ij (keeper of days) in November of 2017.

For more on his work with the Maya, see www.JaguarWisdom.org, or follow him on Facebook at Jaguar Wisdom.

Dance of the Sun Goddess

Pagan Folkways of the Baltic Coast

Kenneth Johnson

Chicago, Illinois

First Printing. 2024.

ISBN: 978-1-959883-24-1
Library of Congress Control Number on file.

Cover design by Wycke Malliway.
Edited by Becca Fleming.
Typesetting by Gianna Rini.

Published by:
Crossed Crow Books, LLC
6934 N Glenwood Ave, Suite C
Chicago, IL 60626
www.crossedcrowbooks.com

Printed in the United States of America.

More by Kenneth Johnson

Flight of the Firebird: Slavic Magical Wisdom and Lore
(Crossed Crow Books, 2023)

Witchcraft and the Shamanic Journey (Crossed Crow Books, 2022)

Jaguar Medicine (Mystical Jaguar Productions, 2017)

The Mayan Prophecies: The Renewal of the World 2012-2072
(Mystical Jaguar Productions, 2012)

Mayan Calendar Astrology (LUCITA Publishing, 2011)

Mythic Astrology Applied: Personal Healing Through the Planets
(Llewellyn, 2004)

Jaguar Wisdom: Mayan Calendar Magic (Llewellyn, 1997)

Mythic Astrology: Internalizing the Planetary Powers
(Llewellyn, 1993)

Contents

Foreword

When I first heard of *The Dance of the Sun Goddess,* I was intrigued because my dad was the son of Lithuanian immigrants. Albert adopted me when I was a young boy, so I do not have any personal close blood ties to the Baltic people, as far as I know. However, I grew up around older, adopted Lithuanian relatives who occasionally conversed among themselves in their native tongue. I remember walking in on my Aunt Alma one afternoon as she was listening to songs in a language that I did not understand. My dad and his relatives rarely spoke of their Baltic heritage, but it was an ever-pervasive presence.

As I began reading this book, I was struck by its importance not only to people of Baltic descent but to all polytheists as well as anyone interested in comparative religion. In our contemporary Pagan culture, we tend to emphasize Southern European concepts. This is understandable to some extent. For those of us who were raised in non-Pagan households, classes in classical mythology were usually our first extensive exploration of polytheism. We may have read comics presenting a fictional version of Thor, or heard of an equally fictional version of Voudoun while watching horror movies, but it was in high school where the majority of us studied the mythologies of ancient Greece and Rome in depth.

As a result, it is often assumed, especially by those new to Paganism, that we all share similar beliefs and perceptions of the universe. Consider, for example, the Triple Moon Goddess. As a Saxon Pagan,

I cannot tell you how many times I have been met with a "deer in the headlights" look from someone when I mention that, for me, the moon is a masculine presence. However much you may love Artemis, Diana, or Selene, the fact is that a moon goddess is not a universal Pagan belief. There are no universal beliefs in Paganism. Indeed, the fundamental quality of Paganism is the understanding that another person's deities and world view may be as valid as your own. Even the concept of Mother Earth falls apart when we cross the Mediterranean and arrive in Egypt, where the Earth was perceived as masculine and the sky as feminine!

We see some of this diversity in the Germanic beliefs of the English and the Norse, of course, where the moon is "male" and the sun "female." And now, Kenneth Johnson presents us with the religion of the Baltic region. Like other Northern Europeans, these people also revered a masculine moon and a feminine sun. Johnson draws upon a rich heritage of Baltic folk songs to reconstruct details of the pre-Christian religion of the Latvians and Lithuanians. It is once again a living religion that has been revived by people, predominantly of Baltic descent, today.

The author begins with a presentation of Baltic cosmology as envisioned in the World Tree. It is an image common to many Pagan cultures, but Johnson goes further and describes it as something within us (microcosm) as well as an external construct (macrocosm). Johnson shows us parallels between the Baltic World Tree and similar constructs in other cultures. This kind of insight is found throughout the book. Johnson does not limit himself to listing the beliefs of the Latvians and Lithuanians, he encourages the reader to think about those beliefs and how they might apply to a personal spiritual practice.

In the book, we are introduced to the storm god Perkūnas, the earth mother Žemyna, the moon god Mėnuo, and, of course, the sun goddess Saulė, as well as many other Baltic gods and goddesses. Here the book includes "magical workings," which are essentially simple observances to honor the deities. This is another way Johnson pushes us to think about how we apply our beliefs to our daily lives. For example, to honor the fire goddess Gabija, he suggests bringing a candle with you when visiting friends and lighting it to give them the gift of fire. As I read this book, I found myself considering again and again how I can infuse more meaning into my own Anglo-Saxon spirituality.

The magical workings appear throughout the book. In the section describing the Baltic holidays, there are customs and traditions that honor each season. *The Dance of the Sun Goddess* is not merely a scholarly examination of a regional Pagan religion, it includes a wealth of material for anyone who might feel drawn to honor the old gods of the Amber Coast. Kenneth Johnson's own passion for the subject is what really gives life to this book. It is a book about what used to be, and yet also a book about what still lives today and will continue on into the future. As if to clarify any question as to whether the book is intended for practical application, Johnson includes an appendix with more than two dozen magical sigils.

This book is important because it presents a Pagan path that has been largely overlooked, despite the fact that the Baltic people were arguably the last Pagans to be crushed by the spiritual genocide that swept across Europe. Johnson chronicles that history in the last chapters of this book, describing the final resistance against the oppression of the Teutonic Knights in the fourteenth and fifteenth centuries.

The Dance of the Sun Goddess is essential reading for anyone who would practice Baltic Paganism, but I would encourage others to read it as well, regardless of your personal path. What I regret is that this book was not written while my dad was still alive. Dad would have loved to have seen this tribute to his ancestors and their culture. I hope you will enjoy it as much as I did.

Alaric Albertsson

Author's Note

Inasmuch as I am not of Lithuanian or Latvian heritage, one logical question—logical, at least, to the contemporary Neopagan community—is why I should find that remote corner of Europe known as the Baltic to be worthy of devoting my time and energy to an entire book on the subject of its ancient Pagan ways.

My answer is that the Baltic is of major importance to all students of mythology, folklore, and Pagan philosophy.

When I wrote the first edition of the book which has recently been republished by Crossed Crow under the title of *Flight of the Firebird,* my background research kept referring to the myths and legends of the Baltic regions as well as to the nearby Slavic lands which were the principal subject of my book. Again and again, I found myself fascinated with the Baltic material, as well as drawn to its unique qualities. While scholars of European mythology—especially at the University of California Los Angeles, where Balts such as Marija Gimbutas and Jaan Puhvel had held the dean's chair in such subjects—are aware of the importance of Baltic myth, the general public is not, and to the best of my knowledge, the book which you now hold in your hands is the first full-length study of the subject to be published in English.

The family of languages which we know as Indo-European is a global phenomenon now. It includes ancient Sanskrit and modern Hindi as well as almost all of our European languages—whether Romance, Germanic, Slavic, or Celtic—except for a few outliers such as Basque,

Estonian, Finnish, and Hungarian. Indo-European languages in many ways dominate the world (though, sadly enough, this has come about largely through conquest and colonialism). But all of them are descended from a single source, a long-forgotten language which scholars have reconstructed as Proto-Indo-European, and which was spoken on the steppes of Russia and the Ukraine c. 3000 BCE. This original language had its own religion, and this vanished faith has been the origin of all our Pagan mythologies—Greek, Latin, Norse, Celtic, Slavic, and Baltic.

It is a Baltic language, Lithuanian, which is the closest living relative to the original Proto-Indo-European language, and not only have truly ancient linguistic traits been preserved in Lithuanian and its close relation, Latvian, but the ancient Pagan traits of Proto-Indo-European mythology have been preserved as well. Baltic mythology is a shining window into an ancient worldview which lies at the foundation of all our Pagan myths.

A good example of this window into ancient Pagan philosophy can be seen even in the title of the present work: *The Dance of the Sun Goddess*. We have become accustomed to thinking of the sun as a male god. But the simple fact is that most early speakers of Indo-European languages regarded the sun as a goddess rather than a god, except in the Mediterranean, where more ancient sun gods and moon goddesses prevailed even after the introduction of Indo-European languages. Norse myth is a good example of a Sun Goddess paradigm, and there is reason to believe that sun goddesses were known in Celtic mythology as well, but it is only in the Baltic that we see the Sun Goddess in her full glory as Saulė, one of the most popular deities throughout the Baltic region which is sometimes known as the Amber Coast.

Not only do the Baltic regions contain some of the oldest mythological themes which appear in all our Indo-European mythologies, but they also contain echoes of even older myths, stretching back into the Neolithic era (c. 9000-3000 BCE). During these five or six thousand years, Europe was the home of a civilization comprised of farming villages, some large and some small. But these villages produced many of the most impressive monuments of ancient Europe—the barrow mounds and stone circles that have captivated our collective imagination and given rise to so much speculation.

Much of this speculation has to do with the very nature of Neolithic society as well as its religion, for many see the Neolithic as a matriarchal society characterized by peace and prosperity. While it is true that some scholars have dismissed the proliferation of female figurines found in Neolithic archaeological sites as "possibly just children's dolls," and while the Ice Man found preserved in a Swiss glacier casts some doubt on just how peaceful the Neolithic really was, former Dean of Old World Archaeology at UCLA Marija Gimbutas—who was Lithuanian by birth—is almost certainly correct in pointing out that the largest collections of such female figurines are to be found in buildings which had a religious purpose.

> *It is in the Baltic that we find the strongest evidence of goddesses from the Neolithic period, with theriomorphic (and thus clearly ancient) figures such as Laume, protectors of the household such as Laima and Gabija, and tribes of goddesses such as the Mothers.*

While I had anticipated that I would find these elements in Baltic myth, there were a few pearls I discovered that were thoroughly unanticipated. I discovered a folktale that is known throughout the world—even in North America and perhaps in Africa as well, but which has its clearest and most elaborate version in the Baltic.

Another unexpected gem was the discovery of an example of euhemerism—the idea that the gods are based upon mortal human beings whose deeds were exceptional. This idea has been thoroughly rejected by modern scholars, but in the Baltic, we may find a genuine example of a mortal woman who became worshiped as a goddess.

One of the most unusual features of Baltic Paganism is the way in which it was preserved. There are no epics such as *The Iliad* or *The Odyssey* or the Mayan *Popol Vuh*, no compendiums of riddling esoteric knowledge or profound stories like the Nordic *Eddas*. Though we have a few rude comments from Christian missionaries who perceived every facet of the local lifeway as "demonic," the opponents of ancient Baltic religion never described it in detail, as Spanish chroniclers did with what they regarded as the "demonic" myths of the Aztecs and the Mixtecs.

Instead, the ancient Baltic way was preserved in folk songs.

Known as *dainas* in Latvian or *dainos* in Lithuanian, these folk songs tend to be quite brief. The most common metric form is only four lines long. Though there are longer folk songs that deal with myth, it is not entirely inaccurate to imagine an entire mythology preserved in *haiku*.

Clearly, this has its delights. But in creating this book, I found some of those delights difficult to access. Almost none of the *dainas* and *dainos* have been translated into English, and the few translated pieces that are to be found are clunky and awkward, the productions of scholars whose intention was to illustrate a point rather than to touch the poetic heart of the Pagan Baltic path.

Balts themselves have continued to cherish their folk songs throughout the ages, and many collections of them exist on the Internet now. Folk groups that perform the ancient songs are extremely popular among Baltic Neopagans. All, however, whether merely collected or musically recorded, are in their original language. The use of Internet translation programs and dictionaries brings you a sense of the verses, though it gives you none of their poetic sensibilities or their musical rhythms.

I have not hesitated to rework the lumbering translations which constituted the original material with which I worked. My hope has been to restore to them, in English, some of their poetic magic. How far I have succeeded, I do not know. I only hope that I have preserved at least a small portion of their musical cadence as well as their pithy and sometimes unexpected depth.

One thing regarding which a decision was necessary: In this book, god names and place names are typically written in Lithuanian, partly because the greatest wealth of general material about the Pagan Baltic is in that language, and partly because Lithuanian is the closest living descendant of the Proto-Indo-European language which gave birth to so much of European mythology and which makes the Baltic material so important to the study of Pagan Europe in general. But the best of the truly mythic folk songs tend to be Latvian *dainas*. Rather than twist the structure of a song, I have left the names in their original Latvian form, which I hope will not cause undue confusion.

It is my hope, someday, to bring out an entire book of translations from the Baltic folk tradition, close in spirit to the original, and enhanced with commentary on the deep Pagan philosophy which these songs so beautifully embody.

Kenneth Johnson

Part I: The World Tree

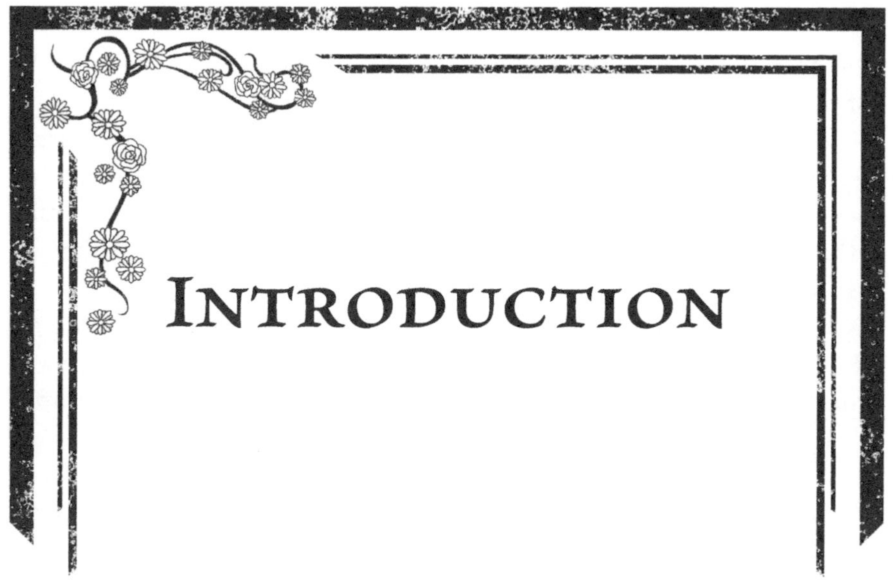

Introduction

The eastern shores of the Baltic Sea were known in ancient times—and are still known today—as the Amber Coast. The region is now the home of various nations—Estonia, Latvia, Lithuania, and eastern Poland—and civilized life has wrought its changes to the landscape. Pines and conifers now dominate among the cities and towns. In ancient times, a different woodland commanded the Baltic shores. The Amber Coast held portions of a truly vast forest that stretched from Russia, all across central Europe, and into the British Isles, even as far as Ireland. It is known to geographers and geologists as the *Hercynian Forest* and was made up largely of deciduous trees such as oak, linden, maple, and elm; poplar, hornbeam, aspen, and birch; hazel, ash, and willow. Most people regarded the forest as a fearsome place. At times an almost impenetrable tangle broken only by swamps, its human inhabitants consisted largely of outlaws and "witches."[1] It was home to badgers and martens, beavers and bears; to squirrels, hares, the lynx, and the boar; to the elk and, until the end of the Iron Age, to wild horses. The giant species of cattle known as *aurochs* lived there, and so did the European bison. It is no wonder that Hansel and Gretel easily became lost in their own part of the great Hercynian Forest, or that their surroundings filled them with fear. There were many birds as well; the folk songs of the Baltic people speak of the singing of partridges and grouse, ducks and geese, larks and cuckoos, nightingales and storks. The song of the cuckoo was believed to be prophetic to those who were capable of understanding it.

The Baltic is a moody sea. In the winter, it is stormy and gray. Sometimes, close to the land, it freezes over (as I myself have witnessed). In the summer, its waves can dance like the waves of any other sea, and the sun can light the crests of the waves with flashes of silver.

But there is gold beneath the flashes of light, a gold that washes to the shore along the Baltic's eastern coast and gleams in the sand—a gold that has often made the fortunes of this remote corner of Europe.

It is a gold called *amber.*

There has always been amber. This petrified golden resin was here before human beings walked the earth. Amber is the resin of pine trees which grew some sixty million years ago. The shores with "amber pine" forests sank beneath the sea, emerged again, then sank again during the slow passage of geological ages. The pine resin, petrified by time, was washed up in huge masses by the sea on what are now the south-eastern shores of the Baltic—and it still exists in quantity along the shores of Poland, Lithuania, Latvia, Estonia, and Russia. The first Paleolithic hunters who sought their game along this coast knew it well, as did their various successors upon the land.

To ancient Europeans, amber was a substance of the sun itself, shining and endowed with magical powers. As precious as gold, it was widely sought by the "civilized" south. For the Baltic area, it became a key to prosperity and a link with rising central European cultures and with Mycenaean Greece. It is mentioned in Homer's *Odyssey*: The King's palace was resplendent in copper, gold, amber, ivory, and silver, and Penelope received a necklace of amber and gold, "like the Sun."[2]

The beginnings of a transcontinental amber trade marked the beginning of the Baltic Bronze Age. Amber was demanded by rising central European cultures and by Mycenaean Greece. When central Europe established commercial relations with the Mycenaeans sometime before or around 1600 BC, the amber trade rapidly reached an amazing volume. The Amber Coast was known to central Europeans who paid for amber with the most precious bronzes they produced and with gold ornaments, some of which were imported from as far away as Ireland.

At the beginning of the Iron Age, central European cultures mediated between the amber gatherers of the Baltic and the early Celtic Hallstatt culture in the Alpine area and the Etruscans in Italy. Astonishing quantities of amber beads and pins threaded with amber are found in the Hallstatt graves and the Etruscan graves of central Italy.

From the classical authors, we learn how greatly amber was valued and desired. And then there are the amber objects which are to be found in Rome and its provinces: beads, vases, cosmetic jars, lamps, human effigies, sculptures of lions, panthers, dogs, goats, tortoises, dolphins, snails, and birds.

Roman imports into Prussia, Lithuania, and Latvia are quite impressive: many thousands of Roman coins, in addition to pots, fibulae, glass beads, bronze vessels, oil lamps, and bronze statuettes.

And yet, amber beads were extremely rare on the Baltic coast itself. To the amber gatherers, the substance was apparently so common that they yearned for more exotic ornaments.

After the fall of the Roman Empire, Baltic trade with the south diminished, but it did not entirely cease. The amber route continued to be used in the fifth and sixth centuries. Numerous golden Roman-Byzantine coins from as late as 500 CE can be found along the Amber Coast. Imported objects from the new "barbarian" kingdoms took the place of imports from the former Roman Empire.

A letter from the great Gothic king Theodoric in Italy to the Baltic tribes thanks them for their gifts of amber. It is the last known ancient text which mentions the magical golden substance.

Though Greeks and Romans paid dearly for their jewelry made from the amber of the far north, they seem to have had very little idea of who lived on the Amber Coast or what their culture was like. Herodotus, the "father of history," makes brief mention of a people called the *Neuri* who may—or may not—have been the Balts, while the Roman writer Pliny the Elder bumbles and fumbles badly about the very nature of amber and cites the voyage of a far traveler named Pytheas, who may—or may not—have traveled as far as the Baltic. Another Roman writer, the historian Tacitus, does somewhat better—and for good reason, as his father-in-law was a provincial governor who administrated parts of Germany that were not too far away from the Baltic shores, which Tacitus referred to as *Aestia.* Several centuries later, Swedish Vikings who lived not far away and had a Baltic coastline of their own came to know the inhabitants of the Amber Coast fairly well—not because they wanted to understand them, but because they raided and enslaved them—or sometimes simply killed them.[3]

Despite the amber trade and the resulting prosperity it brought to the Baltic-speaking peoples of the Amber Coast, the people themselves remained a relatively unknown, marginal society.

Yet sometimes it is in the margins of the world, far away from the march of empire and the epicenters of history, that the greatest cultural treasures are to be found.

The United States provides at least two notable examples which come immediately to mind. In colonial days, the Appalachian Mountains were a frontier region, the westernmost margin of Euro-American settlement. In time, adventurous souls from that mountain region crossed to the other side, to the west, where new opportunities awaited. All they had to do to claim it was to brutally rid themselves of the indigenous people who already lived there. But the Appalachians themselves changed little. These "hillbillies in the holler" became a marginal backwater of the emerging United States. And yet here, where nothing ever seemed to change, archaic forms of the English language still survived—many Appalachian phrases and linguistic traits harked back to the days of Shakespeare. Perhaps the most valuable contribution from "marginalized" Appalachia has been its folk music. Here, the traditional English and Scottish ballads survived in a form more ancient and pure than in their countries of origin. Collected by Francis James Child in the mid-nineteenth century, Appalachian folk songs are among the genuine treasures of American culture.

The Spanish-speaking population of northern New Mexico dates back to 1693, when those who accompanied the expedition of Don Diego de Vargas took root there, founding a number of villages to the north of Santa Fe, New Mexico. These settlers were marginalized by poor communications with Mexico, raids by the Navajo, and the mountain environment itself. They too maintained a way of speaking which was archaic in the extreme. If the inhabitants of Appalachia sometimes spoke with phrases and intonations from

Shakespeare's time, the villagers of Hispanic New Mexico were still speaking the Spanish of Cervantes until quite recently. This author vividly remembers participating with his fellow citizens of our village each spring to clean out the public irrigation ditches which we called *acequias*, though the rest of the Spanish-speaking world knows them as *zanjas*.

The Baltic peoples, another marginal society, possessed a treasure even richer than their amber, and it too was based upon language. The Eastern Baltic languages—Old Prussian, Latvian, and especially Lithuanian—are the closest living relatives of Proto-Indo-European, the original language to which so many of our Pagan European mythologies owe some of their most primal and fundamental ideas. Speakers of Proto-Indo-European traveled from the steppes of Central Asia into India, where they developed the Sanskrit language, the source of so much of the world's spiritual philosophy. They traveled west into Europe as well, and the languages they spawned were the Latin-based languages such as Spanish, Portuguese, French, and Italian, and the Germanic languages such as English, German, and Norse, as well as Slavic and Celtic languages. But it was the Baltic languages, also part of the Indo-European language family although marginalized by their region's geography, that maintained the closest linguistic relationship to original Proto-Indo-European, the parent language of them all. Isolated by their remote location in the north, the people of the Baltic practiced a Pagan faith—the last "formal" Pagan European religion, which survived as Lithuania's official faith until 1386 but persisted in the villages for more than three hundred years afterward—which remained the closest living relative to the original mythology of those long-ago ancestors who spoke the Proto-Indo-European language, a tongue whose linguistic descendants now dominate the globe.

It's a familiar story, one often told. Beginning with the arrival of the first farmers about 7000 BCE, Old Europe was a peaceful place, a land of villages that lay nestled gently in parts of the mighty forest which had been cleared and developed for agriculture. This Neolithic European society was matriarchal, led by wise women who worshiped goddesses of fertility and peace, and whose rituals were devoted to the changes in the year and the growth of the crops.

Then, about 3000 BCE, Old Europe was invaded by warriors from the eastern steppes, bloodthirsty patriarchs genetically damaged by an unquenchable desire for rape and pillage. They descended upon a society unaccustomed to war, riding upon horses and brandishing weapons of bronze, slaughtering the villagers and establishing new and violent patriarchal gods, with mere echoes of the ancient Goddess Civilization surviving in the hidden corners of later mythologies.

And the descendants of these brutal patriarchs continue to control the world to this day.

A familiar story, often told, an engaging story of wise heroines and ignorant villains.

However, it never actually happened.

Whether or not Neolithic Europe was in fact a matriarchy is unknown; the proliferation of goddess figurines found in Eastern Europe certainly suggests that it was. The concept of a matriarchal Old Europe was first developed by European scholars like Johann Bachofen and Robert Briffault and became part of popular culture with the poet Robert Graves' extraordinarily influential book *The White Goddess* (1948). Graves wrote the book to impress his colorfully eccentric lover Laura Riding. He allowed free rein to his poetic imagination and once told his oldest son that he was surprised that anyone actually believed it was all true.

But that doesn't necessarily mean that he was wrong. The foremost proponent of a matriarchal Old Europe was the Lithuanian archaeologist and scholar Marija Gimbutas (1921–1994), whose series of books on Neolithic Europe had a profound influence on feminist ideology, especially Pagan feminist ideology.[4]

It was an earlier archaeologist, Vere Gordon Childe, who had theorized that the peaceful society of Neolithic Europe came to a violent end with the invasion of patriarchal Indo-European-speaking warlords from the Russian steppes. Childe was something of a mentor to Gimbutas, and it was Marija who first identified the original Indo-Europeans with the Kurgan Grave culture in steppe country that is now part of Ukraine. Time has proved that she was correct.

When excavations at the Neolithic village site of Cernavoda in present-day Romania turned up weapons and battle standards which seemed rather obviously Indo-European, Gimbutas was convinced that this was the evidence she and Childe has always hoped to find—evidence that Old Europe had reached a violent end at the hands of invading patriarchal Indo-Europeans.

But there was more to the story, and most of it remains unknown except to the academic community. Most of the villages which Gimbutas had identified as the apex of the Goddess Civilization of Old Europe were in nations which at that time were part of the Russian-dominated Eastern Bloc. Though Gimbutas, a Lithuanian by birth, was one of the few archaeologists in the United States who could read Russian, the Eastern Bloc wasn't particularly keen on sharing information, and many details about the nature of Old Europe and its transition to the Bronze Age emerged only after the fall of the Soviet Empire in 1989.

In the first place, Old Europe was not as peaceful as had generally been supposed. Weapons and fortifications were known to Russian archaeologists, and while this by no means proved that the Neolithic was not a matriarchal society, it proved that the inhabitants definitely knew how to defend themselves—and had enemies which made defense necessary long before the Indo-Europeans came upon the scene. But the most surprising new information to emerge from better communication with the former Eastern Bloc had to do with the reasons for Old Europe's decline and the arrival of the Indo-Europeans.

Around 3000 BCE, the Indo-Europeans entered an Old Europe which was already fading, though it was not yet dead.

The enemy that was overpowering the European Neolithic was not a warlike patriarchal culture.

The enemy was climate change.

After the end of the Ice Age, Europe entered an unusually warm climatic phase that proved to be beneficial to the first farmers. The nations where Old Europe, according to Gimbutas, reached its cultural apex were present-day Romania, Bulgaria, the western part of Ukraine, and the former Yugoslavia. From about 8000 to 3000 BCE, the climate of that region was as balmy and as perfect as southern California.

Then, everything got colder. The strategies which had worked so well agriculturally for the last 4,000 years were no longer effective. Villages unable to support themselves simply vanished as the inhabitants moved elsewhere in search of better farming opportunities.

It was around this time that the Indo-Europeans made their appearance, though they did not ride in on horseback, killing and slaughtering and drooling for rape and pillage. The warrior artifacts found at Cernavoda were one of a kind. Information sharing with the former Eastern Bloc countries revealed that no other evidence of violence associated with the arrival of Indo-Europeans had ever been found. Cernavoda was an isolated raid; nothing else resembling it existed in the archaeological record.

It is not even clear whether the Indo-Europeans could ride at all. Stables and horse corrals found in the steppes of eastern Ukraine revealed a few horse teeth with bit marks—but just a few. The early Indo-Europeans seem to have been experimenting with riding, but it was by no means common. They traveled west into Old Europe in big clunky wagons, and they traveled as merchants rather than warriors.[5]

To all appearances, they were welcomed when they arrived. And there was a good reason for such welcome. Coming, as they did, from the eastern Ukrainian steppe country, they had a skill which made the difference between life and death to the peoples of Neolithic Europe during this epoch of dramatic climate change: they understood the techniques of cold-weather farming.

It is true that the Indo-Europeans were patriarchal in the sense that men were the heads of families and clans, and their mythology tells us that warriors were indeed respected. But they didn't gain control of the new lands through violence.

They didn't slaughter the wise women of Old Europe.

They married them.

Marija Gimbutas was an honest scholar; near the end of her life, she admitted that she had been wrong about the Indo-European migrations, but no one wanted to hear her. By that time, devotees of her work, such as Merlin Stone and Riane Eisler, had transformed the non-existent patriarchal invasions into a watershed of human history which amounted to a watershed between good (the matriarchy) and evil (the patriarchy).[6] Publishers were making millions as their books—and many others in the same vein—topped the non-fiction bestseller list of the *New York Times*. The last thing anyone wanted to hear was Marija Gimbutas herself saying, "I was wrong." Her recantations were cloistered in academic publications and to this day remain unknown to the general public, which still envisions warrior tribes with bronze swords wreaking havoc upon peaceful villages.[7]

The repercussions of all this for Pagan mythology are enormous. Rather than imagining a distant echo of Goddess Europe hidden in the interstices of an overwhelmingly patriarchal Indo-European myth system, we need to begin envisioning a complex blend of mythic ideas which originated only in part from the Indo-Europeans but just as powerfully from the wise women of Old Europe whom they married. Greek myth—the source of Western literature—is a particularly good example. We can assert that the worship of Zeus and the Gemini Twins, and the Greek vision of the Underworld with its canine guardian Cerberus, were in fact of Indo-European origin—but not much else. Aphrodite, Dionysus, and Athena don't correspond to anything in our reconstructions of the original Indo-European myth system. Instead, these deities are from Old Europe and the Near East. All the Pagan mythologies with which we are so familiar—the Celtic, the Norse, and others—are likewise a mixture of religious elements and ideas, blended together like an exotic brew of tea.

But it is in the Baltic—with its languages so closely related to Proto-Indo-European and with an extraordinary collection of goddesses in its mythology—that we find one of the richest treasure troves of a very early, very ancient Pagan worldview.

One

The Tree at the Heart of the World

The center of the universe is everywhere; it is all around us. There is nowhere we can be that is not, at least for that moment, the center of all things. This universal center, this axis mundi, can be described with many different metaphors. In various cultures around the world, it is called the North Star, the central pillar, the World Mountain, or the World Tree. Perhaps the most important and the most enduring of all these images is the World Tree and the cosmos associated with it.

According to myths throughout the globe, we live in a cosmos of three worlds: Heaven, Earth, and the Underworld. The World Tree, the central axis of the universe, has its roots in the Underworld and its topmost branches in Heaven. This great tree mediates between the worlds and forms a pathway from one to the other.

The souls of children yet unborn—and most especially the souls of future shamans—nestle in its branches, ready to climb down into incarnation. A bird spirit also lives in the branches of the great Tree. Above all, at the apex of the world, like the North Star itself, lives the Lord of the World, perceived as a detached, contemplative Sky Father.

The shaman is privileged to be able to travel up and down the World Tree. It is his road; it is the road between the worlds. It is in the starry sky above as well as in this earthly world—as in the famous Hermetic maxim, "As above, so below." The Milky Way is the celestial path which corresponds to the tree itself, and the North Star is the crown of the World Tree, its heavenly apex. When the shaman climbs the World Tree in his visions, he is traveling the North Star Road. Here he receives transcendent messages or snatches of prophecy, important information concerning the proper performance of rituals. He will communicate these messages to the tribe. Climbing down toward the roots of the World Tree, the shaman takes the fearsome road to the Underworld, where dwell the souls of the dead. He does this for several reasons. Sometimes the soul of a sick person has already started on the hard cold journey to the land of the dead, and the shaman, by pursuing the wandering soul and intervening with it, may coax it back to the land of the living. At other times, the soul of one recently dead may become confused, reluctant to quit his former habitation, or uncertain as to how he should proceed. The shaman assists the ghost of his tribesman by showing him the proper path to the Otherworld and guiding him there.

Thus, the World Tree is of vital importance to the shaman, for it is the symbol of his road, the road between the worlds, the road to the North Star, and the center of the universe. Many Siberian shamans paint representations of the World Tree on their drums, while others decorate the central pole of their tent or yurt like a world tree. Some erect a pole just outside the tent and occasionally, during ritual, they actually climb the pole. The World Tree and the threefold cosmos appear everywhere, in mythologies throughout the world. The religions of Native American peoples are quintessentially shamanistic and often embody shamanic ideas in a very pure form. Take, for instance, the Sun Dance. This ritual is performed by many Plains Indian tribes, sometimes with rather different features. The version given here comes from the Wind River Shoshoni of Montana, Idaho, and Wyoming. A large cottonwood tree is selected to become the center pole of the Sun Dance Lodge. The lodge itself is shaped like a tent or teepee, with twelve support beams. That the Sun Dance Lodge represents the shamanic "tent of the sky" is clear from the terminology, for the central pole is "the backbone of the sky," a Shoshoni term for the Milky Way—which frequently serves as a metaphor for the shaman's path to the North Star. A bison head is fastened to the middle of the central pole, facing west. One of the lodge's rafters, anchored in the forked central pole and oriented east-west, contains a symbolic eagle. The Sun Dance lasts several days. After fasting and prayer, the dancers circle round the central pole of the World Tree. One of the purposes of the ritual is healing, and the clothing of those who seek healing is often left to decay in the sun after the dance is over. The central pole, too, must be left to decay naturally.

The Shoshoni Sun Dance is deeply reminiscent of Siberian rituals involving the world axis, but the same cosmology may be found among urban civilizations as well. The Classic Maya, for instance, conceived a superbly shamanic cosmos. In their tradition, the World Tree is a great ceiba or wild cotton tree. This tree grows from the back of a great crocodile who slumbers in a pool of water at the bottom of the Underworld. The Mayan Underworld itself is perceived as an inverted pyramid of nine levels. Above it is the Earth, the middle world in which we live. The roof of our world is the sky, which is held up by four great spirits called the *Bacabs,* who are sometimes represented as iguanas and sometimes as bees. They stand at each of the four cardinal directions. The World Tree continues up past our world, into the sky, the world of the gods. Heaven is another pyramid, this one pointing upward and comprised of thirteen levels. At the apex of the pyramid or the top of the World Tree is the highest heaven. On the great branches of the Tree wait the souls of those unborn, ready to experience new birth in our world. In the topmost branches dwells a mythical bird called the *muan.*

The similarity between the cosmos of the Maya and that of other Native American or Siberian tribes is evident, but if we are to establish any connection between the shamanic worldview and the Pagan worldview of the Amber Coast, we must identify this same cosmos among European peoples.

In 1220, a learned citizen of Iceland decided to preserve the ancient mythologies of the Norse, the old legends that were fast disappearing as Christianity spread throughout Scandinavia. Snorri Sturluson, though himself a Christian, was also a bard, a lawgiver, and a politician, an erudite man with a great respect for the ancient ways. In a book that history now calls *The Prose Edda*, Snorri details the old Norse cosmos. The center of the world is a great ash tree called Yggdrasil. Its branches stretch over Heaven and Earth, while its roots are deep in the Underworld. There are three such roots, for there are three levels of the Underworld. One of these levels is simply called Hel (the origin of our own word "hell") and houses the ghosts of the dead. Another level belongs to the frost giants, and beneath it, there is a pool called the Well of Mimir, which means "well of memory." Under this pool is buried the head of Mimir the Dwarf, a prophet who knew all things. To drink of this well is to acquire all the knowledge vested in collective humanity. A third level of the Underworld belongs to the gods and houses another pool, called the Well of Urd or "fate." Here live the Three Norns, the wise sisters who weave the fates of humanity. Every day the gods travel on horseback over the rainbow bridge and come to the Well of Fate. Here they meet to hold council.

Beneath the World Tree is a great serpent who gnaws continuously at the roots of Yggdrasil. But the World Tree, watered and tended by the Norns, continues to grow high, into the world of humanity, the middle world which is called Midgard. This world, too, is surrounded by another great serpent, the Midgard Serpent. The middle world was fashioned from the body of a great giant called Ymir; his domed skull is the dome of the starry sky. Four dwarves, one at each of the four directions, hold up the sky. Above our world, at the top of the World Tree, is Asgard, the land of the gods—though in fact the Norse heaven has three layers, including the kingdom of the Elves. The gods have their palaces at the top of the World Tree, where a great eagle—as among the Siberians and the Shoshoni—also resides.

The mythologies of the Maya and the Norse, though widely separated in terms of geography, share features that are too similar to be coincidental. They derive from a single source, and Siberian beliefs indicate that the common source is shamanism. The religious practices which comprise shamanism are clearly of extreme antiquity; they were in existence before human beings began to walk west from Siberia to Europe and east from Siberia to the Americas.

Though the Norse example brings us into the European cultural sphere, we may be left wondering whether or not the Scandinavian countries were unique, anomalous, and somehow different. Were they more deeply shamanic than other European peoples?

Although it is true that the Norse retained one of the most powerful and striking shamanic worldviews of all Europe's pre-Christian peoples, they were not alone in that worldview. We can find evidence of the same complex in other mythologies as well. An Irish story tells us how the hero Finn MacCool became a poet. He went to study the bardic arts under an old fellow who lived by a pool that bubbled up beneath a great hazel tree. Hazelnuts dropped from the tree into the pool, where they were eaten by a salmon. Hazelnuts were symbolic of wisdom, and thus this salmon was the wisest creature in the world. The old man instructed young Finn to catch the salmon of knowledge and cook it for his master, but not under any circumstances to taste it himself. Finn dutifully caught the salmon and cooked it—but the grease splattered on his thumb, which he quickly placed in his mouth. From that moment on, all Finn had to do was place his thumb upon his tooth and he was instantly able to understand all things. We may easily recognize the great hazel tree as a World Tree—in fact, some Celtic myths specify nine hazels and place singing birds in their branches. The pool at the bottom of the hazel tree is the Well of Memory, and the salmon may represent the same primordial wisdom as is symbolized by the Mayan crocodile or Norse serpent.

Pagan Baltic Sigil for The World Tree

In Latvian mythology, the World Tree is called the "Tree of Dawn" (*Austras koks*) and is said to stand upon an island or rock in the middle of the ocean. It reaches to the sky, which is variously known as Sky Mountain, Silver Mountain, or Ice Mountain. The central axis of the world is sometimes a World Tree and sometimes a World Mountain, or, in this case, perhaps it is both.) At the top of the tree is a cuckoo bird, which was regarded by the ancient Balts as a prophetic creature. Though many heroes have spent their lives searching for the tree at the center of the world, it was said that no mortal eye has ever beheld it—only the gods can see it.

But there are some sources which give us reason to believe that there were some magical individuals—the shamans of the Baltic lands—who could indeed climb the Tree of the World and reach the heavenly realms, like shamans everywhere.

One of the most charming peculiarities about Baltic Paganism is that some of our best information comes not from dry and clumsy chronicles, but from folk songs, called *dainas* in Latvian and *dainos* in Lithuanian. Some of them stretch back far in time; they cannot be accurately dated, and all we really know is that they preserve knowledge and lore from the most ancient days. We shall encounter quite a lot of such folk poetry in the course of this book. Here is the first such poem, a Latvian *daina* about climbing the World Tree to the land of the Gods.[8]

I had a rose of many colors.
In the garden I carefully planted it.
It grew so thick and tall
That it reached the very sky.
On the petals of the rose
I ascended up to Heaven.
There I saw a son of God,
And he was saddling a colt.
Hello, hello, you son of God!
Have you seen your father and your mother?

In Latvian mythology, there was indeed a sky god named *Dievs* who lived at the top of the World Tree, and he had two sons, the Latvian equivalent of the Greek Gemini twins and Vedic *Aśvins*, who rode on horses through the sky, so our inadvertent shamaness with her magical rose clearly knew whom she was supposed to find at the top of the tree. But for the moment, there is more to be said about the World Tree itself.

Simon Grunau (c. 1470–c. 1530) was a priest, born and raised in Prussia when it was under the control of a controversial band of "crusaders" called the Order of Teutonic Knights. He preached in a city which was then known as *Danzig* but is now called *Gdansk*, in present-day Poland. Between 1517 and 1529, he composed a work called the *Prussian Chronicle* (*Preussische Chronik*), which dealt with the people whom history knows as the "Old Prussians" and who spoke a Baltic language.

The first individual known to make an attempt at converting the Old Prussians to Christianity was Adalbert of Prague in 997. The Prussians killed him. In 1166, two Polish dukes made another try at Christianizing the Pagan Old Prussians. But the Prussians led the Polish army deep into the primal forest to one of the swamps that dotted the landscape, drowning many and slaughtering the rest.

In time, the Order of Teutonic Knights became involved, staging a "crusade" against the Old Prussians, which was launched in 1230. In the introduction, we may have absolved the Proto-Indo-Europeans from pillage, rape, and genocide, but these "Christian crusaders" turned out to be expert at such patriarchal skills. The so-called "Prussian Crusade" lasted for sixty years. By the time it ended, there were very few Old Prussians left, though some people today still claim an ancestral heritage from Old Prussia. The language, however, was lost; only fragments remain, and quite a few of them were preserved by Simon Grunau. As for the Teutonic Knights, they took control of Prussia and founded their own state there—which, of course, was what they'd been aiming for from the very beginning.

Grunau describes a sacred place called *Romuva,* in a Prussian province called *Sambia,* a narrow peninsula which protrudes out into the Baltic Sea just to the south of Lithuania. Romuva, he said, was the principal temple or shrine of the Old Prussians, and it was dominated by a giant oak tree, perpetually green and sanctified by three idols representing the gods Perkūns, Potrimpo, and Peckols—a kingly thunder god, a harvest lord, and the god of the Underworld respectively. Before the oak tree burned a perpetual flame, and the sanctuary was tended by *waidelinns,* young women who were similar to the Roman Vestal Virgins. Sacred to Latvians and Lithuanians as well as the Old Prussians, a *kriwe* or Pagan priest whom Grunau described as the *kriwe* of *kriwes* (Lithuanian: *krivių krivaitis*, Latvian: *krīvu krīvs*), the highest priest of all, presided over this most powerful sanctuary of the cosmic World Tree.

Simon Grunau is the problem child of Baltic mythology. Some scholars regard Romuva as a fictional place, a product of Grunau's imagination. But Grunau was not the first writer to give an account of Romuva. One other source mentions Romuva. Unfortunately, it is just as quirky and dubious as Grunau's version.

In 1326, a certain Peter von Dusburg, a monk and a member of the deeply Christian but genocidal Teutonic Knights, wrote a chronicle which describes Romuva as the most sacred place of all the Balts. He claims, illogically, that the name Romuva is based on "Rome." In his account, the *kriwe* of *kriwes* was a kind of Pagan pope. His messengers were recognized by a certain rod they carried. He guarded the sacred flame and could look into the destiny of deceased followers. He received one-third of any booty taken by Pagan warriors who fought against the Teutonic Knights. To von Dusburg's description of this Pagan holy place, Grunau added the oak tree, the trinity of gods, the resounding term "*kriwe* of *kriwes*," and the attractive young ladies.

There is a great deal which is obviously quite wrong with both von Dusburg's account as well as with Grunau's.

First of all, both writers explicitly assert that Baltic Paganism had a complex hierarchy with the *kriwe* of Romuva at its apex. This is not true. The Pagan Baltic faith was decidedly democratic. And if this "*kriwe* of *kriwes*" were such an influential person, why is he never mentioned by any of the various Teutonic Knights who left accounts of the Prussian Crusade?

And apart from the rather vague description of this sacred place as lying on the peninsula of Sambia, precisely where was it? The Teutonic Knights never found it, even after they had gained control of the entire region. Modern archaeologists have never found it either.

And yet there are historical echoes which suggest that there might be some truth to it all, even if von Dusburg and Grunau both muddled and exaggerated Romuva's importance. For example, the Treaty of Christburg prohibits converted Prussians from inviting sorcerers to their funerals to observe the journey of the deceased person's soul, as the *kriwe* of *kriwes* was said to do. The Teutonic Knights assert that there were those who collected a third of the booty from warriors as an offering to the gods, another custom claimed to have been practiced by the great *kriwe*.

Though the idea that the name Romuva was based upon Rome is laughably silly, there is a Baltic root word *ram* or *rām*, meaning "calm," "serene," or "quiet." Various words derived from this root are common in the names for places that were regarded as an *alkas* or sacred site, for no inappropriate noise was ever allowed at such locations. The word *kriwe* has a historical precedent as well, for it is derived from *kreivas,* meaning "crooked." Therefore, *kriwe* might be a term for "a crooked stick" (*krivulė* in Lithuanian), which, according to Peter von Dusburg, was the most important symbol of the high priest's power.

In my own opinion, however, it is the triad of Gods mentioned by Grunau which provides the strongest evidence that there is more than fiction and fantasy behind his chronicle and that of von Dusburg.

Romuva Sanctuary

Grunau provides us with a picture of a banner which he calls the "Flag of Widewuto." This is Grunau's eccentric spelling of a name which can be rendered into modern Lithuanian as *Vaidevutis,* who was supposedly a king of the Prussians in the sixth century CE, and whose brother was the first of the "*kriwe* of *kriwes.*" Whether these individuals ever really existed is speculative—no one knows. But the flag is of interest to us.

The Flag of Widewuto

The banner depicts the three Gods who were said by Grunau to have been worshiped at Romuva. From left to right, they are Peckols, Perkūns, and Potrimpo.

Perkūns is the best known among these deities, and in this book, we shall often meet him in his Latvian and Lithuanian incarnations, usually under his Lithuanian name, *Perkūnas*. He was known throughout the Baltic as the god of thunder, as well as lightning, storms, rain, fire, and mountains. In social terms, he was the cosmic arbiter of law and order. His tree was the oak, which was the sacred tree of Romuva itself. He was a god of fire, and the sacred flame of Romuva burned in his honor. On the banner, as represented by Grunau, he appears as a rather angry-looking fellow with a tangled black beard and a crown of fire. He rode his chariot through the sky, casting thunderbolts like the Greek Zeus, the Vedic Indra, and Norse Thor. In fact, the *per* in his name is linguistically linked with the name *Thor*. His home, as well as his chariot, is in the sky.

Potrimpo was a god of earth, grain, and crops. He is depicted on the Flag of Widewuto as a cheerful-looking young man wearing a wreath of grain ears. Grunau tells us that snakes were his creatures, and this seems to point to the ring snakes which commonly lived in Lithuanian houses and were regarded as protectors of the home. Fresh water and running streams were associated with him as well. It has been said that Prussians would pray to Potrimpo, pour hot wax into water, and predict the future based on the shapes taken by the wax.[9] We can also think of him as a god of spring, happiness, abundance, cattle, and grain. Clearly, his domain is earth rather than sky.

Peckols is called *Patollo* by Grunau and seems to have been known under a variety of names. He was the lord of the Underworld and the dead and is usually believed to have been both angry and evil. His Lithuanian name was *Velnias.* On the banner, he was portrayed as an old man with a white beard and a white headdress. Terrifying and ruthless, he would haunt and taunt the living if they buried their dead without the proper sacrifices. It is said that he was still worshiped as late as the 1600s.

This triad of deities has its parallels elsewhere in the northern European world. For example, the three barrow mounds at Gamla Uppsala in Sweden are said by Snorri Sturluson to contain the bodies of Odin, Thor, and Freyr, imagined as kings who in time became gods. Thus, we have a triad similar to that of the Baltic: A shamanic Underworld god (Odin and Peckols), a thunder god (Thor and Perkūnas), and a benevolent harvest lord (Freyr and Potrimpo).

As we have seen, the shaman, for whom the World Tree is a kind of cosmos, lives—at least in their physical body—upon this earth. And yet they can climb the World Tree until they reach the sky, the realm of Heaven, or they can venture into the darker realms beneath the roots of the tree, to the Underworld where the dead are to be found.

As a cosmos, the World Tree is made up of three separate worlds: Heaven, Earth, and the Underworld.

Perkūnas, a sky god, travels in his chariot through the realm of Heaven.

Potrimpo, who presides over the harvest and the springs of fresh water which feed it, is a god of the Earth.

Peckols, ruler of the dead and their realm of the afterlife, is the god of the Underworld.

To the Norse, the World Tree was a yew or ash; to the Greek cult of Orpheus, it was a poplar; and to the Celts, it was a hazel tree.

To the Balts, the World Tree was most often an oak tree, though some *dainas* and *dainos* also mention the birch, the linden, or the apple tree. At Romuva, the gods of Heaven, Earth, and the Underworld were worshiped at a mighty oak tree. Romuva appears to have been a model of the cosmos itself.

There may have been something very real behind Grunau's muddled account of Romuva. While he may have been thoroughly expert at his catechism, it seems unlikely that he would have known anything about the shamanic cosmos he described so vividly in his *Prussian Chronicle*. Someone had informed him about the rudiments of the Baltic cosmos, at least.

All the same, we shall leave him to the judgment of historians. For us, there is a matter of much greater importance to discuss.

The World Tree is not only a mythic portrait of the cosmos. It is a portrait of the human being.

The cosmos is not only all around us.

It is within us.

To the Pagan Balts, trees and flowers, groves and forests, stones, and hillocks, and waters were endowed with miraculous life-giving forces. They brought blessings to human beings by healing diseases, safeguarding them against misfortunes, assuring good health, and—of vital importance to an agricultural society—watching over the fertility of the land. Sacred places in nature were carefully guarded, and the "ignorant"—especially Christians—were forbidden to enter sacred forests or groves. No one was permitted to cut trees in such forests or to fish in sacred springs. As we have already noted, such places were referred to as *alkas*. The root word *alk* means "protected" or "invulnerable."

Oak, linden, birch, maple, pine, and spruce were among the most miraculous trees. Medieval records mention sacred oaks consecrated to Perkūnas or sacred linden trees consecrated to Laima, the Goddess of Fate. A stick from an ash tree, a twig of juniper, elder, willow, or any green bough was regarded as an effective weapon against evil spirits.

Forests had their own goddesses and gods. Medeinė (the name comes from *medis*, "tree") was the Lithuanian forest goddess, while in Latvian folklore we encounter a "forest mother" and a "forest father."

Trees were something quite special, highly evolved beings whose energy field, more than all other animals and plants, comes closest to the human condition. There are some smaller plants, such as the *Dryopteris* fern, which are highly charged with healing energy, but in general, it is the trees that hold pride of place as potential friends and allies from the plant kingdom. All trees are positive. They are truly much closer to us humans than any of the animals can ever be. We are like trees. The difference between us is that trees are more evolved than we are. Though this is not directly attested in any Baltic source, Slavic shamans who lived along the Baltic coast sought out trees as their spiritual teachers; they used their tree teachers to help them see within the body of a human being; they used the vision of the tree to study the "esoteric body" of the anxious and the ailing, and thus to diagnose problems and receive information regarding cures.

Present-day Slavic healers insist that if we are to derive the greatest benefit and knowledge from working with trees, we must be aware of their seasons. The birch, for example, is the earliest tree in the forest to leaf out in the spring, and that is its power time. Work with a birch in the spring. Pines, on the other hand, love the sunlight and hold the warmth very nicely; working with pines is best in the summer. The fir trees are calm and quiet and give us tranquility, so one should work with them later in the year, starting in the autumn and continuing throughout the winter. It is the same with the spruce.

In Baltic philosophy, one's liver and lungs are the organs which constitute the essential principle of life itself. There is an aspect of the soul known as the *dušia*, which has its focal point in the lungs. The *dušia* can be thought of as a "material soul." When our life is over, it must walk the dark road to death along with the body. But there is another aspect of the human soul, the *vėlė*, which is vested in the liver, and which also includes such symbolic correspondences as breath, spirit, warmth, and water. The *vėlė* is a living power which does not depart from the earth when a person dies. It is reincarnated—not only in other human beings, but also in trees, flowers, animals, and birds. It leaves the body as a breath, a vapor, and finds a new lodging, sometimes in plants, animals, or birds. It was said that sometimes it would issue directly from one's mouth in the shape of a butterfly, a bee, a mouse, a toad, or a snake, or it might grow out of the mouth of a young girl in the shape of a lily. Often, the *siela* would be reincarnated in trees: men's spirits in oaks, birches, and ash trees; women's in linden and spruce. At the time of one's birth, a specific tree is assigned to every person, and it is filled with the same life forces as its human counterpart.[10]

Hermetic philosophy and Hindu yoga have instilled within us the idea that incarnation as a human being is the highest form of rebirth that one can achieve. The Pagan Baltic had a very different concept. All of nature is sacred; therefore, no stigma is attached to being reincarnated as a flower, a bird, or an animal. And since trees are in many ways more evolved than mere humans, reincarnation as a tree may be considered a very high level of incarnation. It is no wonder, then, that Slavic folk healers sought out trees to be their teachers; they may have regarded themselves as apprentices to former human healers or teachers who had reached a higher degree of evolution.

The World Tree is a macrocosm. It is we ourselves, human beings, who are the microcosm, for the World Tree is within us. We have a trunk—our legs and torso. We have branches—our arms. And we have the leafy crown of our hair on top of it all.

This Tree of Life exists within all of us. In an earlier book, I discussed my Russian teacher who believed that his ancestral tradition acknowledged three centers of power. One of them is in the head and governs our intellect, our intelligence. One of them is in the heart and is the seat of our feelings, our emotions. The third one, in the abdomen, was a center of magical or shamanic power. The firebird, a common figure in Slavic folklore—and at one time perhaps a god—is the energy which can fly to the crown of our own inner tree and enlighten the mind.

The concept of three inner centers may very well be a much more ancient system than India's seven chakras, for it has a correspondence in the three worlds of shamanism—Heaven (our Mind Center or crown), Earth (our Heart Center), and the Underworld (our Center of Shamanic Power).

Students of Chinese medicine, or Qi Gong, will already have recognized that these power centers are identical to the three inner or bodily power centers in the ancient Taoist system of mind and body. All of them are described as "cauldrons." The Mind Center, associated with our consciousness, occupies approximately the same position as the *ajna chakra* or "third eye" in Hindu yoga. The Heart Center is associated with our breathing and our respiration. The Life Force Center, usually called the *dan tian* or "Lower Cauldron" and located in the abdomen or sometimes lower down, is the most important of the three. Here is where the greatest amount of *qi* or vital life energy is stored, and from whence it circulates through the body; this center is also the focal point of our sexuality.

This shamanic concept of three centers within the human body can be found in the Celtic tradition as well, and here, as in China, they are referred to as "cauldrons." The story of the magician Taliesin tells us of a Cauldron of Poetic Inspiration which is kept under the watchful eye of the witch Ceridwen. This appears to be the same cauldron that is mentioned in the old Welsh poem called *"Preiddeu Annwn"* as having a place in the Otherworld—and tradition tells us that the poem was written by none other than Taliesin himself. The Irish god Dagda possessed a cauldron which was always full, dispensing its abundance to all who were worthy. In time, this Cauldron of Abundance became associated with St. Brigid, whose pantry was never empty. Before Brigid became a saint, she was a goddess, and it is appropriate that a goddess should be the keeper of the Cauldron of Abundance. Finally, there was a Cauldron of Death and Rebirth in the possession of the hero Bran, who figures in the Welsh *Mabinogion*.

While it is never directly said that these Celtic cauldrons are within the human body as well as in the mythic world, it is not difficult to make the translation. The Cauldron of Poetic Inspiration is the Mind Center, while the Cauldron of Abundance is in the Heart and the Cauldron of Death and Rebirth is in the abdominal and genital region, symbolizing the Underworld where shamans experience death and rebirth and thereby gain their magical powers.

The Baltic region was converted to Christianity by the Teutonic Knights and, therefore, is predominantly Catholic in present times. But the Slavic countries that surround the Baltic-speaking peoples are typically Eastern Orthodox, and here we find that the tradition of the three inner centers has come to play a role in the practice of *hesychasm,* a meditative discipline which owes a great deal to Byzantium and the Greek Christian center of Mt. Athos. Hesychasts meditate upon icons in order to awaken or enhance certain spiritual qualities. With his prominent bishop's hat or large glowing halo, St. Nicholas is the saint who rules the Mind Center; Russian schoolchildren and even college students sometimes keep a small icon of St. Nicholas with them when they take important examinations. Mother Mary holding baby Jesus awakens the Heart Center, while a saint who is relatively unknown outside of the Eastern Orthodox world is associated with the Life Force Center. Given its close proximity to the Slavic lands, it is likely that Baltic shamans and magicians were familiar with the three inner centers as well.

As we shall see, the Baltic goddesses and gods were frequent travelers upon the World Tree. And if we are microcosms of the macrocosmic World Tree, then the goddesses and gods are traveling within us as well. It is time to meet some of them.

Part II: Goddesses and Gods

Two

HEAVEN

THE SKY FATHER

Sky gods are contemplative rather than active, or so religious scholars assure us. In Baltic mythology, this is certainly true. The Sky Father, called *Dievas* in Lithuanian and *Dievs* in Latvian, is more of a concept than a personality.

Pagan Baltic Sigil for Dievas

Baltic religion is pantheistic. All things are God. Sky Father is the singular Divine Being who is the center of the universe, but the universe which he embodies is filled with a host of divine beings who are simply archetypes of the various aspects which his wholeness, his oneness, encompasses. Whether it be Perkūnas driving through the sky in his chariot and casting thunderbolts, or whether it be the goddess Laima who weaves the fates of human beings or the goddess Gabija who symbolizes the sacred fire of rituals and ceremonies, all these divine entities are but manifestations of the one essence we call Sky Father.

His name itself is derived from the ancient Proto-Indo-European word *deiwos,* which means "celestial" or "shining." The sky is infinite. There is nowhere that the sky is not. Sometimes he is called *Dievas Senelis* (Old Man God), and sometimes *Dangaus Dievas* (God of Heaven). He has a fair number of titles in the Lithuanian language: *Aukščiausiasis* (the Highest One), *Visagalis* (All-Knowing), and *Praamžis* (the Eternal One) are among them.

Because he is inactive and does little, there seems not to have been a cult devoted to Sky Father, or any sacred places that were associated with him. He does, however, have his own plant, a species of artemisia known as *Southernwood,* which in Lithuanian is called *Diemedis,* the God Tree.

Even the folk songs dedicated to him are often philosophical rather than personal:

God was, God remained,
God gave wise advice:
God gave leaves to trees,
God gave corn to the fields.[11]

And another one in the same mode:

Whose mountains, whose valleys,
And whose the spacious fields?
God's mountains, God's valleys,
And God's the spacious fields.[12]

Yet the human imagination, by its very nature, seeks to personify things, and in a Pagan faith which is recorded primarily in folk songs, it would be unusual if the contemplative Sky Father were not given a human personality.

It is said that he lives on Sky Mountain and that he has a farm there. As we have mentioned previously, the center of the world can be described as a World Mountain as well as a World Tree (Mount

Meru in the Hindu tradition is probably the best-known such World Mountain). But Sky Father's home is also known as *Silver Mountain* or *Ice Mountain*—images which may represent stars or snow. Occasionally he descends from his mountain to look in on the human world, making sure that everyone is acting in accordance with universal rightness or cosmic law (the Sanskrit *rta*). He enjoys taking part in the solstice festivals and harvest rituals. He drives down in a chariot and is often accompanied by various female companions (*Santa* here is a common Latvian name):

Slowly, slowly, God rode to the widow's field,
He didn't want the wind to lift up Santa's skirt.[13]

His visits to the world below are welcome ones and full of magic:

Slowly, slowly, God rode down the hill;
The daughter of the Sun was opening the gate;
The gloves of the stars were in her hand.[14]

When a farmer needs help or advice, Sky Father may join with Saulė the Sun Goddess, or Laima, Goddess of Fate, dressed like farmers and their wives. They walk the farmer's fields with him and help him with his problems. When Sky Father plays the role of an old man, teaching people the right way to live, he dresses in the rags of a wandering beggar, heals people, and practices magic.

He is helpful to human beings:

I too have walked the road.
If God came with me,
My feet did not get wet,
And the horses did not sweat.[15]

Darkness in the field, darkness in the field,
Where did you find a friend?
God was my friend on the road,
And Laima was my guide.[16]

THE THUNDER GOD

Dievas may be the source of cosmic righteousness and order, but his role is contemplative, meditative. It is the Thunder God (Lithuanian *Perkūnas*, Latvian *Pērkons*) who actively enforces the divine law of Dievas, whose son he is often said to be.

Perkūnas is a god of lightning, thunder, and storms. As the active force who keeps the cosmic law of Dievas in order, he is a symbol of triumph, creative force, and courage. His thunderstorms clear the environment of evil spirits. He cares only about honor and justice. He holds money in disdain; he is not the god to pray to if you are seeking prosperity.

He is depicted as a man in the prime of life, or sometimes middle-aged, with a long, thick, red beard (the color of fire). His most common weapons are a double-sided iron axe and javelins or arrows which correspond to the thunderbolts that he throws. He rides through the sky in a fiery, two-wheeled chariot which is sometimes said to be made of red iron and is often said to be drawn by goats (like the Norse Thor or Celtic Taranis), less often by horses. In the sky, his chariot is what we would call Ursa Major or the Big Dipper, which was often perceived by ancient Europeans as a wagon of sorts.

Perkūnas dwells on high hills or mountains: He is essentially a sky god and a member of the trinity of Romuva. In most myths, Perkūnas's wife is Žemyna, the Earth Goddess. The number of his sons and daughters differs from one source to another, but it is clear that his family included sons who symbolized various aspects of thunderstorms (such as thunder, lightning, and lightning strikes) and daughters who symbolized various kinds of rain.

Perkūnas possesses many weapons. In addition to his axe and arrows, he is also said to wield a sledgehammer, stones, a sword, a club, and an iron or fiery knife. He is sometimes said to be the creator of the weapons, but sometimes it is said that his arsenal was created with the help of the heavenly smith Kalvelis.

An important function of Perkūnas is to fight Velnias (in Latvian, *Vilns*), the Lord of the Underworld. He is sometimes considered to be the antithesis of Perkūnas. But Velnias always manages to escape from Perkūnas. He hides in trees, under stones, or turns into various animals: a black cat, dog, pig, goat, lamb, pike, cow, or a person.

Perkūnas' tree is an oak—it is the only tree that can absorb thunder and channel it into the ground without harming itself. Jesuits in Lithuania in the sixteenth century were horrified to discover that Lithuanians were still worshiping Perkūnas, especially in the form of old oaks. He had his sacred groves, where eternal fires were kept burning, as at Romuva. If for any reason such a fire was extinguished, it was re-ignited with sparks from a huge stone as soon as possible. Such places were often fenced off or surrounded by a moat. Hills or trees said to have been touched by Perkūnas' hand were considered sacred, protected from evil and pestilence.

Magical Working

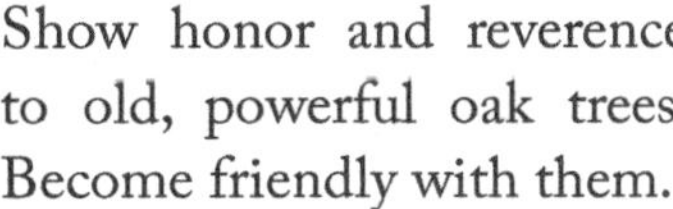

Show honor and reverence to old, powerful oak trees. Become friendly with them.

The 1500-year-old Stelmužė Oak. Said to have been sacred to Perkūnas.

Perkūnas' sigil, shown below, protects people and houses from misfortune. In addition, it is used when signing a contract and during drinking rituals. You can place this symbol on a door or window to protect your house from spells.

Pagan Baltic Sigil for Perkūnas

The day of the first spring lightning is considered a magic time; immediately after the first spring storm, the flowing waters have healing properties.

His day is Thursday, which is also the day of Thor—anyone familiar with Norse mythology should by now have recognized that these deities are one and the same. Thursday was considered a likely day for thunderstorms and rains but was also said to be favorable for weddings.

Magical Working

To honor Perkūnas on a Thursday, put a lit candle in the window.

Most modern urbanites get married on a weekend so that their friends will be off work and able to attend. If circumstances permit you to get married on a Thursday, it is auspicious to do so.

When eating and drinking during summer solstice ceremonies, pour a bit of beer on the ground in honor of Perkūnas.

In Latvia, people sacrificed black calves, goats, and roosters to Pērkons, especially during droughts. Villagers came to these sacrifices to eat and drink together, after pouring beer onto the ground or into the fire for him. The Latvians also sacrificed cooked food to Pērkons before they themselves began to eat.

Latvians wore tiny axes on their clothing in his honor, a talisman not unlike the hammer of Thor.

His special day was June 24, the day after the summer solstice celebration of Rasas.

Perkūnas is a delight to linguists and students of comparative mythology. His name can be reconstructed in Proto-Indo-European as *Perkwunos*, and his name is closely related to those of other thunder gods in many Indo-European mythologies: the Vedic Parjanya, who is another name for Indra; Celtic Taranis; Germanic Thor; and Slavic Perun. The Greek Zeus takes over the functions of both Dievas and Perkūnas and though his name is more closely related to that of Dievas, he is sometimes said to be *terpikeraunos*, meaning "one who enjoys lightning."

As we shall see when we come to consider the goddess Aušrinė, there is one very well-known *daina* that makes it sound as if Perkūnas or Pērkons is married to Saulė, and such a union is indeed implied in several sources. He is also sometimes said to be the husband of Žemyna, the Earth Goddess. In general, however, the wife of Perkūnas is commonly said to be called Perkūnatete, whose name, like that of her spouse, is derived in part from the Proto-Indo-European root word *Perkwunos,* which refers not only to an oak tree but to a wooded mountain.

Perkūnatete is sometimes said to be one of those who, like "the sons of God," wait upon Saulė and heat her sauna when she returns from her daily ride through the sky. Sometimes said to be the mother of Perkūnas, Perkūnatete is more often said to be his wife. She is frequently represented as an oak tree with a cleft that resembles the vagina, the cleft indicating that she has been struck by lightning. She even catches fire now and then if she is lightning-struck when the wood is dry. This brings her great pain. Her pain, however, is archetypally symbolic and may represent either the pain of childbirth or the pain of an experience with a bad lover. If her lightning-stricken agony results in childbirth, her uterus will first cause her to scream in pain but eventually burst into laughter as a new child is born. If her pain is caused by a bad experience with a lover, it can only be healed by good sex, coitus as a *hierosgamos* or "sacred marriage."

THE SUN GODDESS

Yes, in the Baltic, the sun is a goddess, not a god. We are accustomed to sun gods and moon goddesses; this is part of our classical heritage. In Greece, the sun was always a male figure, while the moon was the very archetype of the feminine principle (ask any astrologer). The Romans adopted the Greek pantheon, and the influence of Greece and Rome has been so foundational to Western culture that we simply take the matter for granted.

Not only is Saulė the Baltic solar goddess, but she's also Indo-European. We have already spent some time speculating that the Indo-Europeans may not have been the brutish tribal warlords that we always thought they were, and it may come as a surprise that the earliest Indo-Europeans looked upon the sun as a goddess. Saulė's name is derived from a reconstructed Proto-Indo-European word *Sehaul,* and though the Greeks and Romans preferred a male sun god, the Norse also knew the solar orb as feminine, though she doesn't play quite such an important role in their mythology as Saulė does in the Baltic. In the sad Irish love story of Dermot and Grania, the name of Isolde's predecessor, Grania, suggests that she too had her origins as a solar goddess.

Pagan Baltic Sigil for Saulė

The Baltic Saulė is one of the most important deities of the region, and she is the queen of the folk song tradition, the subject of more *dainas* and *dainos* than any other Baltic deity, even the majestic Perkūnos. She is, after all, responsible for all life on earth. The Lithuanian word for "the world," *pasaulis,* and the Latvian word *pasaule,* both mean "a place beneath the sun."

Some say that she is the daughter of Dievas himself, Others say that the divine smith Kalvelis, the Baltic Hephaestus, fashioned Saulė and tossed her into the sky.

Saulė is an attractive goddess. She and her daughters dress in shawls woven with golden threads; Saulė wears shoes of gold, as well as a golden scarf and belt, gold rings, and gold ribbons, though sometimes she is garbed in red, silver, and white. She is also depicted in a silver, gold, or silken dress and wearing a gleaming golden crown. She even has a gold boat that she uses as one of her means of transportation. In Latvia, where her name is *Saulė,* she is often associated with the color red, symbolizing the fiery nature of the sun.[17]

She likes to dance and is said to dance on a silver hill in her golden or silver shoes.

Saulė, dancing on a silver hill,
Silver boots are on her feet.
She brings joy to all who see her
As she dances and leaps in the clouds.[18]

And here is another poem in the same vein:

Saulė, what did you see,
flowing in the middle of the air?
I saw God playing,
I saw angels dancing.[19]

She is fascinated by belts or girdles, whether of silver or gold. There are a fair number of *dainas* that speak of her passion for such precious, glittering apparel.

Why does Saulė weep so much,
every night in setting?
Her golden belt
Has fallen to the bottom of the sea.[20]

A dense growth of linden
Is next to the Sun;
Saulė can be sold,
She has such desire for a silver belt.[21]

Silver linden grew
On the edge of Saulė's path;
She has a lust for belts,
She can be bought any evening.[22]

In these tales, male deities, especially the ones known as the *Sons of God* (Dievas), prepare a sauna for her when she returns home to the World Tree at night, but they also spy on her and hope to see whatever they can see. If they are lucky, she might let them whip her with a besom of birch in the sauna, which was a common custom in the Baltic, in Russia, and other far northern lands.

But her most important task is her daily journey through the sky. Her daughter Aušrinė—Venus as the Morning Star and Goddess of the Dawn—lights a fire when her mother rises and helps to ready her for her journey.

Saulė takes a long time to rise in the dawning of the day because before she begins her journey, she must act as a mother and comfort the orphans of the world. But in time, she takes her road through the sky. She drives a shining chariot of copper or gold, pulled by horses who never tire, never rest, never even sweat. Her horses are variously described as white, gold, silver, or shining with a diamond color. Sometimes they are said to be yellow, and sometimes they are said to blaze like fire. Their hooves and bridles are of gold as well, though some *dainas* say that the horses themselves are bay-colored.

While some folk songs simply say that the Sons of God help Saulė to prepare and care for her horses, other *dainas* imply that the Sons of God are, in a certain sense, the horses themselves—that they transform themselves into her steeds, pull her chariot, and then metamorphose back into a more human form when the journey is done and they begin to heat up her sauna. In any case, these Dieva Dēli (Sons of God) are also known as the *Ašvieniai* or "horsemen," and are the same gods as the Aśvins of Vedic India, who ride across the sky in horse-drawn chariots. We know them in ancient Greece as the Dioscuri or Gemini Twins, Castor and Pollux.

When the sun rises or when it sets, it is said to be like a wreath of roses or a single rose in bloom. In the fullness of the day, Saulė is said to resemble a daisy, a wheel, or a rosette. When the sun was setting, the ancient Lithuanians said she was like a golden wheel or a golden circle, rolling down a mountain. The red ball of the setting sun is often portrayed in Baltic art as a ring, a falling red apple, or a crown.

The Rosette of Saulė at Mid-Day

When she returns home at the end of the day, it is her other daughter, Vakarinė (Venus as the Evening Star), who makes up her bed in the evening.

But where is her home?

There are a number of myths about it, and wherever we find myth, we find a *daina* to describe it.

You little ones don't know
Where Saulė sleeps at night:
In the middle of the bend of the sea
At the tip of the golden reed.[23]

And another, very similar *daina*:

Young boys don't know,
Where Saulė sleeps at night:
She lies in the midst of the sea
On a rock at the end of the Golden Reed.[24]

There are many different myths and stories about Saulė's nocturnal activities. Most of them say she lives in the Tree of Dawn on its rock in the middle of the ocean, though some say she lives in a castle with silver gates at the end of the sea, a dwelling "in the east." Or perhaps she simply sinks to the bottom of a lake and sleeps, like a baby, in a silver cradle. Others say she wakes up in a red tree in the morning, and that she herself is glowing red, but this resting place of hers may be the Tree of Dawn.

Those who claim she lives in a castle in the east tell us that she holds the golden reins of her horses and washes them in the sea while sitting on top of a hill. Those who sing that her home is in the World Tree claim she removes her girdle or belt and hangs it in the World Tree. This is when the lustful Sons of God begin to spy on her.

But before she sleeps, she weeps. Why? One *daina* has already told us that she weeps when her belt or girdle falls into the sea. Another *daina* gives us no particular reason for her sorrow, but tells us:

Behind the hill
Is where the red berries grow.
Saulė is weeping
Every evening when she sets.[25]

It was commonly said in the ancient Baltic that red berries found upon the ground were the tears of Saulė, dried and hardened.

Yet another *daina* says:

Why is Saulė crying so much?
The silver boat drowned in the sea.
Don't cry, darling, God will make another,
From gold, from copper, from silver. [26]

This leads us to a much deeper understanding of Saulė and her role in the cosmos of the Pagan Baltic.

For there are those who say she's a night traveler and never sleeps.

Whoever said Saulė sleeps at night, he lied.
Did the Sun rise where it set yesterday? [27]

At night, it is said, her solar chariot is transformed into a silver or a golden boat. In the evening, she hangs her gleaming crown upon the World Tree, climbs into her boat, and sails away.

She passes Sky Mountain as she journeys out into the sea, and there are many scholars who believe that "the sea" is not simply the Baltic but the "celestial ocean," the realm of stars and planets, the cosmos itself. Sometimes she seems to be sailing on the Daugava River. This river is real enough in the worldly sense, and now goes by the name of the *Dvina,* but the river seems to have had a celestial counterpart, and this is the Daugava upon which Saulė is sailing in her golden boat. It marks the boundary between this world and the Otherworld. Saulė is ferrying the souls of the dead down the Underworld River, for if day is life, night is death, and Saulė is the goddess who walks the Road of Life and Death, and she is the spirit of rebirth.

Celestial Rivers

It is not unusual, in traditional cultures, for sacred portions of the landscape to have a counterpart in the sky as well. The Daugava traveled by Saulė at night is clearly the river that leads to the Otherworld rather than the earthly river called Daugava or Dvina. It is probably the Milky Way, known all over the globe. In 2001 and 2002, I accompanied archaeo-astronomer Francis Warther in a study of the Wailua River temple complex on the Hawaiian island of Kauai. The ancient Kauai calendar begins on the autumnal equinox, September 21, and c. 1000 CE, the Milky Way would have been directly above the Wailua River, with the Great Rift of the Milky Way over the division of the Wailua into two separate streams at midnight. Warther found that the various temples along the Wailua corresponded accurately to constellations along the Milky Way, the most important of which was clearly the two "Birthing Stones" which would have been precisely beneath the Gemini stars. The Great Rift in Sagittarius has symbolized, in many cultures, the place where the souls of the dead enter the Otherworld, while the opposite point along the Milky Way, the Gemini stars, symbolize the "birthing place" where souls return to the world. Important sacred places along the worldly Daugava River may have corresponded with constellations along the Milky Way.

If Saulė's daily journey through the cosmos is full of mystery, her relationships are a complete muddle; tangled and impenetrable. The motif of the "celestial wedding" appears in various *dainas* and is usually seen as a wedding between the "sons of God" and the "daughters of the Sun," Aušrinė and Vakarinė. But some scholars have seen the celestial wedding *dainas* as referring to a union between Saulė and Sky Father himself.

The most common stories, however, claim that Saulė is the wife of the Moon God, *Mėnuo* in Lithuanian and *Mēness* in Latvian. They are the mother and father of the planets: Aušrinė and Vakarinė (Venus), Indraja (Jupiter), Sėlija (Saturn), Žiezdrė (Mars), Vaivora (Mercury), and Žemyna (Earth).

Saulė is a kindly and benevolent Goddess. She shines down upon all of us. Her warmth ensures the fertility of the earth. She is the guardian of the world's unfortunates, especially orphans and young shepherds, and she is one of those who, like Sky Father and the Fate Goddess Laima, may sometimes wear peasant clothing and walk with farmers in their fields to give them good advice. Her festivals took place during her annual changes: the solstices and equinoxes. Her greatest festival took place at Midsummer, of which we shall hear more later on.

The harmless green snakes called *žaltys,* which were often kept in Lithuanian homes as protectors of the household, were sacred to Saulė.

THE MORNING STAR

In Lithuania, both the Morning and Evening Stars are said to be Saulė's daughters, though in Latvia, it is the twins who pull Saulė's chariot who occupy that position. The Lithuanian Goddess of the Morning Star, Aušrinė, is the one who gleans the most attention. She is not only Venus as the Morning Star but also the Goddess of the Dawn—which, of course, is preceded by Venus when it is the Morning Star. We can see this in her name, for as the Dawn Goddess she is called *Aušra,* which is related to the Vedic dawn goddess Ushas and the Greek Eos, the descendants of an ancient Proto-Indo-European Dawn Goddess whose name seems to have been Heusos. Aušrinė has her own sigil, which was used to attract love and beauty into one's life.

Pagan Baltic Sigil for Aušrinė

As we have seen, it is Aušrinė who helps her mother to prepare for her daily journey across the sky. But Aušrinė has servants of her own, including one who guides a herd of cows across the "sea of sky" at night until they reach their morning pasture. This sea of sky must surely be the celestial counterpart of the earthly sea, as we have already learned in regard to the Daugava River. Is this why Aušrinė is called "the Maiden of the Sea"? And this "herd of cows" must surely be the stars, another link with Vedic India, where the stars are also perceived as a herd of cattle in the sky.

In addition to her duties as a sky goddess, Aušrinė also has her links with the ocean and is sometimes called "the Maiden of the Sea," a role she often plays in Lithuanian folk tales. One wonders if this sea, however, is the "sea of sky."

It is said that Saulė, who is very much a beauty in her own right, is nevertheless jealous of her daughter, who is even more beautiful. And Saulė may have a very good reason for her jealousy, for Aušrinė has the same romantic temperament as an Aphrodite or a Freya, and though the Moon God is married to Saulė, he is something of a womanizer and an oaf. He fell madly in love with the beautiful Morning Star; the Moon God cheated on the Sun Goddess with the Goddess of Dawn. (The fact that many *dainos* make Aušrinė out to be Mėnuo's daughter doesn't add consistency or logic to the story, but her parentage is given differently in different sources and, in any case, incest is a common mythological paradigm, whether in Greece, Egypt, or in northern lands.) Perkūnas, the Thunder God, takes umbrage at the Moon God's bad behavior and splits his head in two with an axe or a sword. (This seems to be a somewhat muddled account of the waxing and waning of the moon.) As usual, there is a *daina* about it all:

On the first day of spring
The Sun and Moon were married,
But the Moon rose up before dawn
Because he could not sleep.
He wandered alone in the dark
Until Aušrinė the dawn appeared.
The Moon fell in love.
Perkūno grew angry and vengeful,
He split the Moon's head with his terrible sword.
"How could you cheat on Saulė?" he said,
"Breaking your oath like an unbeliever?"[28]

In any event, Aušrinė somehow manages to stay in Saulė's good graces, and it is said that she and her mother often descended to the Earth together during the time of the summer solstice and danced with mortals, Saulė on a silver hill decked out in red flowers and wearing silver shoes while Aušrinė danced on "a large rock."

Three

EARTH

THE EARTH GODDESS

The Earth Goddess of the Pagan Baltic is called *Žemyna* in Lithuanian; her name is derived from Lithuanian *žeme*, meaning "earth." In Latvian lore, she is, as we shall see, somewhat more complex and controversial. Žemyna is a typical Mother Goddess: She is herself the fertile earth and nourishes all things living, whether plant, animal, or human. Since all that is born of the earth must someday return to the earth as well, she is in some respects a goddess of death, a chthonic deity who receives the souls of the departed as a mother would receive her children.

Pagan Baltic Sigil for Žemyna

Žemyna was widely worshiped throughout the Baltic. The Roman historian Tacitus, who, as we have seen, was better informed about the region than most other Classical authors, tells us that the Old Prussians worshiped the "mother of the gods." In 1605, Jesuit missionaries in

Lithuania complained that huge stones with flat surfaces were believed to be goddesses. Such stones were still being worshiped as recently as 1836, and it was believed that rainwater which collected in the hollows and crevices of such stones had magical properties. In Slavic countries, she was called *Mati-Syra-Zemlya,* "Moist Mother Earth," and, when I was in Russia, I was told that large flat stones were sacred to the Earth Mother there as well. I was also told that Mother Earth's body is made up of the stones beneath us; her bones are the roots of trees and her hair the trees themselves, as well as the grasses which cover the earth. Offerings to Mother Earth were made by these large stones, and more offerings were left among the branches of trees.

Magical Working

When you encounter a large stone with a flat surface, make friends with it. If you find rainwater in its hollows, collect it and use it for magic.

Sometimes it is said that she is married to Praamžis, a manifestation of Dievas, Father Sky. More often, however, she is said to be the bride of Perkūnas the Thunder God. Either way, it is a marriage between Mother Earth and Father Sky, and the earth must be fertilized by the rain and thunder of Perkūnas so that she may produce her abundance.

She is a goddess of the cycles of the year. The vernal equinox is the time when the souls of the dead, who have been upon their earthly sojourn, return to their own world, and a new cycle begins in the world of the living. Žemyna is reborn, emerging from beneath the earth in the form of a young girl. Around April 21 or 22, she reaches her first bloom of womanhood at the festival called *Pergrūbris* in Old Prussian, which symbolizes her marriage to Sky Father as Praamžis. As a married woman, she can now capture the spark of Saulė's heavenly fire, the sunlight, and create new life. In the world of mortals, the time of plowing may begin. Perkūnas sends down his life-giving springtime rain and his bride drinks deeply of it so that she may give birth, may procreate. A member of her own family, the Witch Goddess Ragana, will bring the dead earth back to life—fields that have been empty all winter will blossom again.

Offerings to Žemyna are made at every ceremony, every ritual, from the universal ceremonies of the harvest to each wedding in each humble family. Offerings of thanks are made at the birth of each child, and whenever someone sets forth upon a journey.

From Žemyna I have come
And to her I shall return.
You carry me
And feed me
As I walk upon you
Every morning,
And I kiss you.
Guide me by day
So I can kiss you in the evening.[29]

Magical Working

At every celebration, be it a wedding or a harvest, be sure to spill some beer upon the ground in honor of Žemyna and say a short prayer in her honor before partaking of your meal. Let the bones and scraps of such a meal be buried or burned.

Never spit on the ground. It dishonors Žemyna.

Begin and end each day by kneeling and kissing the earth, remembering that from Žemyna you have come, and to her, you shall return.

In the same spirit, kneel and kiss the ground and say a prayer to Žemyna whenever you begin a journey, and whenever you return.

Though basic she may be to the conduct of life in general, she is not without her mysteries. One of these mysteries is the goddess known as *Māra*.

In Latvia, Māra is the name of the Earth Goddess. Or is it? No one is quite certain who Māra really is.

In many ways, she certainly seems to attend to some of the same business as Žemyna. She is the patroness of all things feminine—children, farm animals, food, even money, and the activities of the marketplace.

She has her connection with the Underworld as well. It was said that when a mortal died, it was Dievs who took the person's soul in his keeping, but Māra who took the body.

Māra was of such importance in Latvia that the region itself (known in those days as *Livonia*) was sometimes called "Māra's Land" (*Māras zeme*). This makes it seem as if Māra was indeed another name for Žemyna.

And yet the ancient inhabitants of Latvia may have disagreed, for they often regarded her as the same goddess as the Lithuanian *Laima*, the Goddess of Fate, whom we shall meet very shortly.

Two of her sigils have survived through the ages.

One of them is a simple cross which may remind us of the symbols of Perkūnas or Saulė. Yet the other is a rippling, zig-zag pattern which somewhat resembles the sigil of Laima.

And there are even some scholars who believe that she was never really a goddess at all. The name, they say, suggests that her origin dates from after the introduction of Christianity and that she is, in fact, Mother Mary. It is clear that in the Mediterranean, Mary commonly took over the functions attributed to earlier mother goddesses. Did the same thing happen in more northerly lands? Did Mary take over the symbolic attributes of earlier goddesses like Laima and Žemyna?

The festival of Māra was called *Māras* and was held on August 15. This is also the day of the Assumption of the Virgin, the major Christian holiday devoted to Mother Mary.

Who came first? Did the worship of Mary take over that of another, pre-Indo-European goddess called Māra, a typical Neolithic Earth Mother? Or did Christians attribute the functions of various and sundry goddesses to their own mother goddess, Mary? Was there ever really a Pagan goddess called Māra?

Someday, in some long lost *daina* or some dusty library, there may come an answer. Until then, we shall simply let it be.

THE GODDESS OF FATE

Like Māra—with whom she may be at least in part identical—Laima is a bit of a mystery. It is not entirely certain who she really is. Some scholars would give her an Indo-European origin. They point out that sometimes she has two helpers who are often described as her sisters and are variously named in different Baltic regions. This triadic structure, it has been argued, links her to the Three Fates of Greek myth or the Norns of Viking legend. Yet sometimes she stands alone, and one of the Baltic's foremost mythological scholars, Algirdas Greimas, believes she is a pre-Indo-European Goddess of the matriarchal Neolithic.[30] As we have seen, the Indo-Europeans didn't conquer the wise women of Neolithic Europe as we once believed—instead, they most likely married them. The activities of our ancient ancestors often show up in mythology as marriages between deities—Indo-European Zeus (whose name is based on the Proto-Indo-European sky god Dyaus) weds Hera, who is clearly a much more ancient Neolithic Goddess. And Laima sometimes—though not always—appears to be the spouse of none other than Dievas (or at least of one of his numerous manifestations), and Dievas is yet another name derived from the Proto-Indo-European root word *Dyaus*.

Pagan Baltic Sigil for Laima

Laima's name is based upon the Lithuanian word *laimė*, which means "happiness" or "good luck." And sometimes that is what she gives us.

Happiness, happiness comes to the son
Who was born in the light.
Laima spun the reins of his life
And soaked them in silver.[31]

At other times, people are plagued with an unhappy fate and a life full of misfortunes.

Laima sits upon the hill.
She weaves the thread of life.
She binds a good mother's daughter
To the son of an evil father.[32]

And yet Laima is more of an administrator of human destiny rather than its author, for only Dievas is omniscient, and the fates of all of us originate with him. Because he cares for righteousness and cosmic law, our misfortunes are more often than not the result of our violation of Dievas' sense of what is right. Life can be like walking up a mountain, in rhythm and in harmony, but it can also be out of harmony, a tumble down the hill where Laima sits weaving.

If Dievas is the ultimate arbiter of human destiny, what precisely is Laima's part in it all? Algirdas Greimas says that Laima knows everyone's destiny, for she is the spinner who spins it, and it is she who must cut the thread. She may not have been the ultimate creator of a mortal's destiny, but she *knows* your destiny, and if you ask her, if you follow her ways, and honor her as the goddess she is, she just might tell you. We have seen that the cuckoo is a prophetic bird, and it is the cuckoo who is Laima's personal animal totem. The number of the cuckoo's calls was believed to predict how long a person had left to live. In the spring, it would also determine how a person would spend the remainder of the year; for example, if a man had no money on him when he heard the cuckoo, he would be poor for the rest of the year.

I heard three cuckoos.
In the light of the day, I trembled.
What is my fate and where shall I go?
And what path will I choose today? [33]

Pagan Baltic religion was not fatalistic. Your destiny can change. You can return to the path of Dievas, of cosmic justice. And Laima just might help you, for she is a friend to humankind. Like Saulė, and sometimes Dievas himself, Laima will dress as an old-fashioned farm woman and come help you in the fields. In spring, she strolls through the fields, blessing the planted seeds, while during the harvest, the abundance of the harvest depends on her. She is often sitting near your hearth, invisible, watching to make sure the family is walking the path of Dievas, the path of righteousness. She often hangs around the hearth and watches to make certain that the family is walking along the path.

Laima is honored at birthdays, baptisms, and weddings. She has a special concern with childbirth and marriage, and she is the patroness of all pregnant women. She will watch over the birth of a child. She has influence over the course that a pregnancy will take and what the delivery will be like. Her weaving determines what sort of personality and talents the newborn baby will have. Lāima knows what the child's financial status will be and when and how they will leave this world. But her primary concern is with birthing; her sisters are more interested in the growth of the child, their adult life, and death. Later in the child's life, however, she will help arrange marriages and oversee weddings.

Magical Working

After a successful childbirth, it is Laima who should be thanked. Even at the end of the nineteenth century, long after the introduction of Christianity, the neighborhood women, family, and friends would gather to sing songs in her honor. Only women could participate in such a ritual, which was performed in the sauna. As in nearby Slavic lands, the bathhouse was a kind of family temple, and births often took place there.

As we have seen, the lives of plants and animals were just as important as the lives of human beings, and a person could be reincarnated as a bird or a tree just as easily as entering another human body. Laima was revered as the patroness of cows and horses. She spun the lives of plants and animals as well as human beings. Laima's sacred tree is the linden.

THE HARVEST LORD

As long as there has been agriculture, there has always been a Harvest Lord. We have already met the Old Prussian deity Potrimpo who was a god of earth, grain, and crops. He is depicted on the Flag of Widewuto as a cheerful-looking fellow, and Perkūns seems to be giving him a dark stare, as befits one who enforces cosmic law and finds the rural joys of Potrimpo a bit frivolous. Like Saulė, he is a protector of the harmless ring snakes who served as creatures of good fortune in Pagan Lithuanian homes. Fresh water and running streams were associated with him as well. He was a god of spring, happiness, abundance, cattle, and grain. In many respects, he resembles the Norse god Freyr. Clearly, his domain is earth rather than sky.

Pagan Baltic Sigil for Jumis

He was a keeper of herds. Milk and grain are dedicated to him, and he is responsible for the agricultural abundance that feeds both people and animals. Since the cycle of growth is associated with the changes of the moon, Potrimpo is deeply connected with the Moon God as well. Baltic Pagans prayed to the Moon God for good fortune. It could even be said that the moon is one of Potrimpo's incarnations, and he is also linked with Saulė, for the harvest cannot grow without the sun.

Fertility, health, and wealth: the good things in life are his domain.

In Latvia and Lithuania, he was known as *Jumis,* and his festival was held around the time of the September equinox. In Christian times, this celebration was known as *Mikeli,* after St. Michael, and is roughly equivalent to the British Michaelmas. This ritual will be described in more detail in a subsequent chapter, but one of the principal acts of the ceremony was the so-called chasing or catching of Jumis; the woman who was known as the best reaper would lead everyone into the fields brandishing a large phallus made of a sheaf of grain tied into a knot and topped with a stone. It is sometimes said that the young women who supposedly served at the shrine of Romuva were devotees of Potrimpo. No wonder he felt like laughing at the serious outlook of Perkūnas and found his grim focus on righteousness to be amusing.

Jumis not only lived in the earth, he lived below it. From the depths of the world, he blessed the harvests above him. Because he lives in the fields, the last of the harvest would be left there for Jumis to dwell in.

His name seems to have been based on *yemo,* the Proto-Indo-European word for "twin." Despite the name, he is clearly a pre-Indo-European god from the Neolithic. Though we know very little about Neolithic religion, it is fairly clear that the Harvest Lord was a deity known to the earliest farmers, who appeared on the European landscape about 7000 BCE. At some point, the ancient god of agricultural abundance received a new Indo-European name, for in Latvian myth, his bounty is almost always doubled, and his name can also signify a "double ear of wheat." When ears of corn grew together on one stalk, they were called *Jumis.* Young sweethearts hunted for such stalks of corn, for whoever found one, it was said, would soon be married. Any fruit or flower which grew in such unusual duplication was called a *Jumis.* It was believed that eating Jumis would cause women or female animals to give birth to twins.

As a double entity, he includes both the masculine and the feminine principle—let us remember that sweethearts sought his blessing when they wished to be married. As he is the lord of each new harvest, he is the growth of human beings as well. This doubling or twinship can be seen in his symbol as well, for half of it points upward toward the light to symbolize the first half of the agricultural cycle and the principle of growth, while the other half points downward, just as the ears of corn will grow heavy and droop in the second half of the cycle, leaning towards Jumis' abode beneath the earth.

THE GODDESS OF FIRE AND THE GOD OF THE SEA

The Goddess of Fire is named Gabija, and her name is derived from the word *gaubti,* meaning "to protect." She is the spirit of the sacred fire of every household and every hearth, and she protects both the home and the family that lives in it.

In ancient times a holy fire (*šventa ugnis*) was kept in tribal sanctuaries on high hills and the banks of rivers, like the perpetual fire which burned at Romuva. Priests stood guard over it. It was not allowed to go out except at the Midsummer Festival when it was extinguished and then rekindled to symbolize the beginning of a new cycle of time. A fire at one of these sacred altars was regarded as the best mediator of prayer. The fire carried the words of our prayers, hopes, and desires to the gods and the ancestors. A story is told of three priests who lived long ago. They tended a sacred fire at the top of a mountain. People came there to confess their wrongdoings, then they held their hands close to the fire for ten minutes or as long as they could tolerate it. This was a rite of purification of the human soul; it cleansed people of their misdeeds.

Eventually, this tradition became a domestic rite centered around the hearth fire of individual homes. Care of the household fire was the responsibility of the mistress of the house. As the goddess Gabija was the protector of the fire that burned at the hearth of every home, so was the mother of the family the protector of the household fire. Thus, it is the mother who, by tending the hearth fire, was symbolically tending "sacred fire" as it was understood at shrines and holy places; she created the link between the family and the world of the gods for whom the sacred fires of holy places had originally burned. She carefully tended the fire and prayed to it to ensure the family's good fortune. At night, she would put the fire to bed, as it were, by covering the charcoal with ashes. Bread and salt were placed next to the fire as offerings to Gabija, and sometimes a bowl of clean water was placed there as well so that Gabija could wash herself. Just as the priests of the ancient shrines had extinguished and then rekindled the fire at the summer solstice, so did the mother at every home. Important family rituals included fire. When a young woman of the family was to be married, she was given fire from her mother's hearth in order that Goddess Gabija might bestow an auspicious beginning upon the new family. In addition to marriage, baptisms and naming ceremonies were performed at the hearth in the presence not only of the parents but, symbolically, in the presence of the ancestors as well.

Magical Working

In ancient times, families often exchanged fire. When you visit like-minded friends, bring a candle with you and light it to give them the gift of fire.

Gabija was perceived most often as a woman dressed in red, though she could also take on the shape of a cat, a stork, or a rooster. She had her dark side. If anyone should stomp, spit, or urinate on the household fire, she just might get angry enough to burn your house down.

In addition to the summer solstice, Gabija had other ceremonial days as well. On February 5 (very nearly correspondent to the Celtic Imbolc), a candle was carried three times around the kitchen table or the fireplace, and the sigil of Perkūnas was marked on the forehead, back of the head, and behind the ears of all family members to protect them from the Thunder God's fiery lightning. On December 6, a pair of horses, representing the Divine Twins or Sons of God, was led around the house to protect it from fire, a ceremony which was dedicated to both the Twins and to Gabija.

Bangpūtys was most likely the God of the Sea. There are so few references to him in Baltic sources that it is difficult to be certain. He seems to have been perceived as austere and unrelenting, the sea in turmoil, as it so often is in the Baltic lands. He has a beard, wings, and—like the Roman god Janus—he has two faces. He is often shown with a fish in his left hand, some sort of utensil in his right hand, and a rooster perched on his head.

It is said that Bangpūtys was the father of the gods of the four winds: Rytys, Pietys, Šiaurys, and Vakaris (the eastern, southern, northern, and western winds respectively).

Bangpūtys was considered a very vindictive god. For example, one story talks of how Auštaras (son of Aušrinė and the Moon God and another god of the easterly wind) was swimming in the sea and Bangpūtys raised a storm, trying (apparently without success) to drown him.

OF WILDERNESS AND LOVE

In a culture where forests are abundant and some of them are considered sacred, a culture where each god and goddess has a sacred tree (honored and decorated by worshipers), and where a tree may even hold the spirit of a beloved ancestor, happy and cheerful in their new incarnation among the other inhabitants of the forest, we would expect to find a deity who acts as guardian of the wild—and indeed we do.

Her name is Medeina, and she is usually depicted as a beautiful young woman, sometimes with green hair. Her sacred animal is the hare; she often romps with the rabbits. Even in the final days of Lithuanian Paganism, when Christianity was gaining a following among some of the people, churchmen complained that there were many—including the Grand Duke himself—who continued to worship Medeina.

Christian chroniclers who had a Latin education often compared Medeina with the Roman Diana. Indeed, the comparison was apt, for there were many similarities. Though beautiful, she had no interest in romantic relationships and steadfastly refused marriage with any other deity, though it is implied that many would have been more than willing.

What she preferred was wilderness. Like Diana/Artemis, Medeina was a huntress, though she protected wild animals more often than she hunted them. As we shall see when we begin to study the Baltic calendar, there were times of the year when wolves could be hunted, and times when they could not—this despite the fact that wolves were considered a very real danger to both people and livestock. The protected seasons of the year may have had something to do with Medeina, who was considered to be their special guardian. Along with the wild hare, the wolf was also her sacred animal. Her concern was not with the hunter but with the hunted. She was not particularly interested in protecting people from wolves; she was interested in protecting wolves from people. It is said that she sometimes took the form of a wolf and that she wandered the woods as a wolf, accompanied by packs of wolves.

Her popularity is clear from the fact that numerous shrines dedicated to her are recorded. One modern archaeologist records five sanctuaries—sacred stones, hills, and forests—that were dedicated to the hare, and presumably to the goddess Medeina. He also discovered no less than ten sacred sites called "wolf footprints," which were large stones that contained hollow spaces resembling the footprints of wolves and which were also most likely regarded as shrines to Medeina.

Magical Working

Though it may be unlikely that wolves are to be found in your neighborhood or anywhere near it, you are certain to spot a wild rabbit or hare every now and then, even in the city. Be sure to greet it with friendship and respect, remembering that you are in fact greeting the goddess Medeina.

Among contemporary Neopagans in the Baltic, Milda the Love Goddess is a favorite. There are many Lithuanian *dainos* devoted to her,[34] and she is praised as young and beautiful, though somewhat lazy, and she is compared with some of the most popular trees, such as the oak, the linden, and the birch. She is a stream of wine, a field of daisies, and a fragrant lily bush. Those enthralled in her worship neither sleep at night, nor work during the day, nor eat with their families, and she is said to be like horses who are dancing in a garden.

You are a green tree.
Why did you grow green,
Why did you grow up?
One's fork, one's top,

If I had single-steel scissors,
It cuts off the top of the blade.
I have two or three wickets left.
Through one gate the sun rises,
Through another gate, the moon rises,
Through the third gate, the sister goes,
High in Vainikai, long-haired.

Here comes the beauty of our Sun,
Here comes the beauty of our sisters.
And where our sister stood
There was a stream of wine flowing.
And where our sister sat
There was a flower bed of roses.
And where her feet stood
There was a fragrant lily bush.
And where her hands lay
There were golden rings that glowed.
Say to the beauty of our Moon,
Say to the beauty of our brother.
And where our brother stood,
There flowed a stream of wine.
And where our brother sat,
There a peony bush bloomed.
And where his horse's legs stood,
There the clover fields smelled.
And where the horse's hands lay,
There the maple leaves were twinkling.

The birch tree is standing still.
No one is harming it.
No one is riding.
The young birch tree is lazily lazy.
The birch tree spent the night.
The birch tree didn't sleep.
Thank you. The birch tree left early in the morning.
I spent the night with a birch tree in the leaves.

In the new nursery, a sedge was growing.
Oh sedge, sedge, who sowed you?
I was sown by a big wind.
Oh sedge, sedge, who watered you?
I was watered by a big rain.
Oh sedge, sedge,
Who plucked you with a scythe?
The most beautiful girls
Put it on my head, on my head.

And yet these *dainos* are of recent vintage (and thus more impressionistic), composed in modern times by Milda's Neopagan worshipers, for she is mentioned nowhere in any ancient text, and there are some academic skeptics who claim that this eminently popular goddess never existed at all.

Milda was first mentioned by a scholar named Teodor Narbutt in his 1835 work on the history of Lithuania—a massive tome comprised of no less than nine volumes. He alleged that she was known not only as Milda but by the rather Greek-sounding name of Aleksota. Her temples, he asserted, stood in Aleksotas, Kaunas, and Antakalnis, a site in the Lithuanian capital of Vilnius, where the Church of St. Peter and St. Paul now stands. According to Narbutt, the month of April was dedicated to her, though contemporary Neopagans celebrate the Love Goddess in the month of May.

From whence did Narbutt draw his conclusions? A teacher from Kaunas had told him that two figurines had been found at an ancient temple dedicated to Perkūnas at the end of the eighteenth or beginning of the nineteenth centuries. Based on the teacher's description, Narbutt concluded that the figurines were those of Perkūnas and Milda. Yet another figurine, this one of bronze was found at the Vilnius Castle Complex and identified by Narbutt as Milda. This, of course, does not explain where Narbutt obtained his information about her pseudo-Greek name, the sites of her temples, or the month of April as her sacred time.

I take no particular stance on the scholars and other critics, but the reverence which the contemporary Neopagan community shows to this Goddess of Love—and the fact that a European culture without a Love Goddess would be a rarity almost unknown elsewhere—demand that she be included here.

Magical Working

Celebrate Milda in May. Take a vacation from work and relax among the flowers and the trees as her contemporary devotees do.

THE MOTHERS

In Latvia, we may find a mythological anomaly of great interest and perhaps of great importance. It is unique to the region, and does not appear in other Baltic societies such as Lithuania or Prussia; nor, indeed, can it be found in any myth system throughout the vast Indo-European world.

This phenomenon is a group of goddesses known, quite simply, as the Mothers (*Māte* or *Mahte*). And when I say "a group," I am referring to no less than sixty or perhaps seventy goddesses.

Given such a large number, any folklorist—or indeed, any casual reader, is likely to assume that the Mothers should no doubt be classified as nature spirits of one type or another, yet all the primary sources assure us that the Mothers are in fact goddesses, authentic deities.

Where do they come from, and what is the meaning of such a plethora of goddesses? Pagan feminists will do doubt rejoice in thinking that here, at last, is the evidence for which they have sought so long—a testimony to the fact that long ago, in the Neolithic era before Indo-Europeans ever appeared upon the scene, European society was matriarchal and all deities were goddesses.

And perhaps they are right. Technically, we do not have any firm archaeological evidence to support the contention of thinkers like Marija Gimbutas that Neolithic society was matriarchal or at least matrifocal. The structure and indeed the very nature of Neolithic social organization remains unknown to us. However, it is worth noting that the Mothers are goddesses who watch over very specific areas of life—ancestor worship and the spirits of the dead, the sea, the forest, the winds. We can be even more specific than that, for there are Mother Goddesses who watch over fields of crops, milk, cattle, mushrooms, elk.

It should be noted that there are no contemplative deities of sky or atmosphere and that the province of the Mothers is entirely of the earth itself, and often of aspects of nature that were demonstrably important during the Neolithic (c. 8000 to 3000 BCE).

Everything we know about the Neolithic strongly suggests that ancestor worship was an important feature of religious life. The great long barrows, granges, and other types of mounds are clearly communal graves for particular communities and also functioned as religious centers, presumably for the worship of the ancestors buried there. And while there may still be some debate about the meaning of the stone circles and other standing menhirs which proliferate throughout Europe and are most famously associated with the British Isles, there is a growing consensus that these massive stones hold the spirits of revered—or perhaps even deified—ancestors. Zemes Mate (Earth Mother) was said to receive the spirits of the dead when folk had passed and were entering the Otherworld. She is often mentioned in connection with other Mothers such as *Velu Mate* (Mother of Dead Souls) and *Kari Mate* (Mother of Graves). Zemes Mate and Kari Mate are associated with the resting places of the dead, guarding their bodies and holding the key to their graves. In the case of Zemes Mate, whose name means simply "Earth Mother," the reference to burial places is quite clear.

The Latvian Mother Earth is clearly the same goddess as the Lithuanian Žemyna, who nourishes all things. But since all things born must someday die, Žemyna plays the same role as Zemes Mate in receiving the spirits of the dead. Offerings to Žemyna were made at every ceremony, every ritual, from the universal ceremonies of the harvest to family weddings.

It is the Latvian Zemes Mate who sometimes goes by the name of Māra, whom we have already met through the medium of the Lithuanian Earth Goddess. Māra also has a connection with the Underworld, for though the Sky God may take our souls at the moment of death, it is Māra who takes our bodies, for we are buried in the earth, and Māra is the earth. As we have seen, Latvia was known as Māras zeme, Māra's Land. This title and her clear identification with Zemes Mate lend credence to the idea that Māra was originally a Neolithic Earth

Goddess, that Mother Mary's attributes were attached to her rather than the other way around, and that Māra's original sacred day of August 2 was moved to August 15, the Assumption of the Virgin, to accommodate the rapid growth of Christianity in Latvia (instigated by the brutal conquest of the Teutonic Knights).

The goddess known as Velu Mate was said to be the Queen of the Underworld, while Nāves Māte (Mother Death) and Kari Mate (Mother of Graves) were also well known. Death was an important matter, one which was ruled primarily by the Mothers, which, once again, fits in with everything we know about the Neolithic.

There are also Mothers who watch over the world of Nature, such as Veju Māte, the Mother of Winds, who rules not only the winds but all weather of whatever quality, Miglas Māte, the Mother of Fog, and Lietus Māte, the Mother of Rain. Juras Māte, Mother Ocean, is the goddess of all the seas and of the vast ocean, while Bangu Māte, the Mother of Waves, will remind us of the male Lithuanian god Bangpūtys. There is Udens Māte, the Mother of Waters, and Upes Māte, the Mother of Rivers.

And in a world of forests and trees, we ought not to be surprised to find a Meža Māte, the Mother of the Forest, who is the guardian of the woods and the wildlife that dwells therein. And though the tradition of the Mothers has survived only in Latvia, it seems clear that Meža Māte is none other than the Lithuanian woodland goddess Medeina, whom we have already met.

Moving from the wilder realms of Nature to the fields of Neolithic farmers, we find ourselves in the world of Lauka Māte, the Goddess of Farmland. From the fields that surrounded the homes of ancient farmers, we move into the homes themselves, where we come across Mãjas Gars, the spirits of the house, perhaps the most important of whom—at least as regards the Mothers—were Pirts Māte, Mother of the Bathhouse or sauna where children were often born and where women held their most sacred rituals, and Uguns Māte, whom Marija Gimbutas recognized as none other than Gabija, the Lithuanian Goddess of Fire and a guardian of the hearth as well as a protectress of home and family.

This, then, was the world of the Mothers, and the possibility is strong that it was a very ancient world indeed.

Four

The Underworld

THE LORD OF THE UNDERWORLD

As a member of the Romuva trinity, the Underworld Lord is shown as an old man with a white beard and a white headdress. Some people think the headdress looks like a turban; but as we shall see, it is an important clue to his personality and his affinity with other deities.

He has many names. In Old Prussian, he is most often known as *Peckols*. Simon Grunau calls him *Patollo,* and there are some who feel this is a different deity altogether, though most believe that Peckols and Patollo are one and the same. In Latvia he is called *Vilns,* and in Lithuania *Velnias*. Both of these names are based upon the word *vele,* which means "the dead," those over whom this god rules and whom he protects. His realm lies underneath the World Tree, and in many ways is a mirror image of our own world. It even has its own World Mountain, Mt. Anapils, and this is where Velnias dwells, just as Dievas dwells upon Sky Mountain in the world above the great tree.

Because he ruled the Underworld, Christians came to associate Velnias with the Devil, though his authentic role in ancient mythology was in fact quite different.

Velnias is a world maker; the world was created by Dievas and by Velnias—the two opposite polarities of life and death working together. But as we have seen, Dievas, the archetypal Sky Father, is contemplative rather than active. It is Perkūnas who acts on Sky Father's behalf, who both creates the world and enforces cosmic justice. Sometimes Velnias and Perkūnas work together in harmony as they continue, eternally, to create and re-create the world. But often, they are at odds with each other. In some ways, Velnias is a bungler—he makes a mess of Perkūnas' efforts unintentionally. At other times, he works in opposition to Perkūnas on purpose. After all, Dievas and Perkūnas represent the law and justice of the world above the World Tree, the world of light and sky. Though Velnias is not by any means the same as the Christian Satan, it is still true that he represents the law and justice of the opposite polarity from the world of light and sky—his world is the world which lies in the tangled roots of the great tree, the world of darkness and the dead. We cannot expect that Velnias and the sky gods will always be on the same page.

Therefore, in many folktales, Perkūnas angrily pursues Velnias, bent upon destroying him. But Velnias always escapes. The rooster who crows at the break of dawn is a servant of the world of light and sky who alerts Perkūnas to the whereabouts of Velnias, but somehow, the Underworld Lord always manages to elude the Thunder God. He hides under stones, in the hollow of an oak, or under a stump. He takes refuge in a swamp, an acacia tree, or in dark places near alders, aspens, firs, and swamp birches. When the Thunder God has passed on his way through the sky, failing to capture the Underworld Lord once again, Velnias emerges from his hiding place and continues with his work.

Sometimes, Velnias can be a friend to humankind. He is a patron of agriculture, hunting, trade, and skilled crafts, in which role he is responsible for the creation of all the tools we use. At his best, he is a god of knowledge, magic, and wisdom, of culture, religion, the continuity of the family, and communication with our ancestors. Note that his gifts are practical and material, the opposite of Dievas' immaterial gifts of spiritual enlightenment and contemplation.

He is a shapeshifter. He can appear as an animal, a bird, a reptile—or a human being. He associates with what we might call the minor goddesses and gods—the spirits of forest and field, the guardians of animals. Because human beings often reincarnate as animals, he is a guardian of creatures, for many of them are in fact the spirits of human beings now dead and thus under his power.

His relationship with human beings is complex and contradictory. Sometimes he seeks our friendship or our help—even our love. He often asks for human assistance in helping him to hide from Perkūnas, but he himself is often the helper—he lends a hand in farming our land, building our houses and bridges, protecting us from outlaws and criminals. He assists blacksmiths and hunters—and even priests! (Here, we should probably understand that he gives his help to priests of the old Pagan faith, those who ritually honor the spirits of the ancestors who are in his keeping.) He loves to listen to mortals playing upon musical instruments. He can appear as a very attractive fellow—he is quite the ladies' man, and they find him irresistible.

And yet his law is quite different from the law of Dievas and sometimes he can cause human beings no end of trouble. He makes fun of our foibles, misleads us, takes control of us, and tempts us or seduces us. Some of his shapeshifting can be terrifying in nature. He can become a destructive whirlwind, a serpent, or a dragon who symbolizes theft, envy, and indolence. He can become a goat, a symbol of sexual lust.

Just before the winter solstice, the life-giving light of Saulė, the Sun Goddess, is at its weakest. At this time of the year, the souls of the dead are here and present in the world—a presence regarding which we shall more to say a bit later on when we turn our attention to the annual festivals. Velnias leads an army of souls to defend her, and upon the winter solstice itself, he and his ghostly troops fight a battle against the powers of darkness and restore Saulė to us for a new birth. He then rides through the world on a white horse and gives gifts to one and all.

In Norse myth, Odin likewise rides on the magical horse Sleipnir and gives gifts. It has been noted that Velnias has more than a few similarities with Odin, as does Volos, the Slavic God of the Dead (and Volos comes from the same Indo-European root word as *veles,* the Lithuanian word for "the dead"). Odin and Volos both wander the world in cloaks of gray, like Gandalf in Tolkien's novels, visiting human homes and performing magic. In Russia, it is St. Nicholas who wanders, cloaked in gray and sporting a long white beard, to perform such feats of magic.

Many of the Pagan Russian gods took on new lives as Orthodox saints and found their way into the artistic tradition of icons. Russians meditate upon icons in much the same way as a Hindu would meditate upon a *yantra* or other religious image. In the icon tradition, attention is drawn to one of the three centers of power in the human body that we have mentioned in Chapter One. St. Nicholas draws our attention to the head, the Mind Center, because he is often depicted in a big, oversized bishop's hat or sometimes with a shining, oversized halo; one can't help staring at them. Russian university students keep an icon of St. Nicholas about them when they must take exams, and Russians in general may carry an icon of St. Nicholas when they travel because he is a wanderer.

The headdress of Peckols or Nicholas, the gray hood of Odin, Volos, or Gandalf, the tangled hair of Shiva—different cultures and even different religions all recognize the same symbolic attributes, for in the end, they are all one, and they all identify such saints and gods as those who have a deep connection with the dead as well as with the living.

THE WITCH GODDESS

If there is one deity of whom we may say with confidence that her origins lie in Neolithic times, long before the advent of the Indo-Europeans and their pantheon, it is Ragana the Witch Goddess. With many similarities to the Slavic Baba Yaga, she is a goddess of death and transformation—the passage from life to death and the passage from death back into life as well.

Her name may be founded in the Lithuanian word *regėti,* meaning "to see," for she is a seeress and prophetess who knows all things. It has also been suggested that her name originates in the Old Prussian *rags,* meaning "horn," and refers to the lunar crescent, for this phase of the moon is her special time—a time where the lunar symbolism of change and constant movement is especially clear to all who gaze into the sky.

It is entirely possible that both root words are relevant to her name and her function. In modern Western civilization, we have been trained by science to believe that there is only one answer, one solution, one possible truth that "scientifically" explains any given phenomenon. Indigenous people, however, tend to see multiple meanings in the same symbolic frame of reference. The moon and the prophetic function are both part of her essence.

Integral Thinking

Indigenous peoples throughout the world perceive mythemes in terms of multiple but associated meanings. For example, B'atz', a day sign in the 260-day calendar of Mesoamerica—which is still kept by the Guatemalan Maya—means "howler monkey" in the K'iche' language if we include the aspirants, but if we simply say batz, without glottal stops, it means "thread." However, in Mayan mythology, the monkey twins are the creators of all the fine arts such as singing, musicianship, and writing, while the most common art form among the contemporary Maya is weaving. Hence a person born on a B'atz' day is said to be a "master of all the arts." Similarly, the day-sign Iq' means "wind," but if pronounced as iq it signifies the moon and a lunar month. People born on Iq' days are known for their ferocious tempers which blow like a hurricane, but if the parents of an Iq' child seek to control the child's temper, they will pay attention to the phases of the moon in order to determine which lunar phases produce temperamental displays in the child, and which phases make them quieter and more agreeable.

She is a goddess of winter, of night, and of death, but also of rebirth. She can destroy and she can heal. She has powers over the fertility of people as well as animals. She can make a woman fertile or infertile, and she can render men impotent by stealing their sexual drive from them. She can curse a farm so that its cattle give no milk. The cycle of menopause begins with the touch of her red wand, which is her special magical implement. Like Perkūnas, she has power over the weather, raising storms or bringing them to quiet, raising or halting the wild wind. Thus, she is a guardian of nature's cycles: creation, growth, decline, destruction. She keeps things in balance. She even controls human population growth: when there are too many people, she can turn them into stones, trees, animals—or perhaps she will simply eat them.

Ragana is a shapeshifter who can take on many forms. She may appear as a beautiful, sensual woman or a blighted hag. She has many animal disguises. She can transform herself into a snake, an owl, a fish, a hedgehog, or even a toad. In addition to hedgehogs, she also has an affinity with goats and mares. Among fish, she prefers the carp and the pike. When she wishes to move swiftly, she flies—in addition to owls, she enjoys the company of magpies and crows. And like a stereotypical witch, she may ride through the sky on a stick, a branch, or a tree stump.

Witches on Ice

Russian magicians have a deep reverence for the powers of water, especially cold water; they like to bathe in it, even in the dead of winter. This practice has filtered down to the popular level, and many Russians enthusiastically praise the benefits of ice water bathing. In the 1930s, a village man by the name of Porfiry Ivanov underwent a spontaneous mystical experience that, in time, made him a well-known spiritual teacher, though in fact he may be most accurately regarded as a master of the Slavic magical tradition...Bathing in ice-cold water was one of his favorite practices, a method for obtaining magical power. His influence on Russian magic has been great and partly accounts for the present popularity of ice water bathing. During World War II, the Nazis occupied Ivanov's home village. The Germans decided to test Ivanov's power. They cut a hole in the ice, stripped him down to his underwear, tossed him in, and forced him to remain in the freezing water for nearly four hours. They became nervous when they noticed that the ice around him was melting, so they pulled him out again, then drove him around, still wet and still in his underwear, on a motorcycle for another two hours. They had to stop because their motorcycles were running out of gas. So they took him to his home. When he stepped down from the motorcycle, he shook their hands and said, "Thanks for the ride." Johnson, Kenneth, *Flight of the Firebird*, Chicago, Crossed Crow Books, 2023.

Ragana doesn't travel alone. She has an entourage of formidable female spirits called *raganas* who are at her service. They enjoy gathering together to bathe, dance, cavort, or simply celebrate in their own fashion. But they don't enjoy being observed by others, especially men. If a man is caught spying on Ragana and her companions during one of their frolics, he will first be devoured by them sexually before they devour him literally. (It is not clear whether he will die happy.) And just as her companions are known as *raganas*, so are the mortal priestesses and devotees who serve her. In Lithuanian folklore, witches fly off to hilltops to rendezvous with Ragana on her sacred night, which, not surprisingly, is the winter solstice. She cuts holes in the ice of frozen lakes at the tops of the chosen mountains, and the *raganas* bathe in the icy water. Concealed by stands of birches—which are Ragana's special tree—they sit and comb out their long, long hair.

It may seem paradoxical at first, but the summer solstice is also one of Ragana's special days. At this time, when Saulė is at the height of her power, Ragana reminds us that nature is mortal and that there is no life without death. She turns back the force of the sun, and from that day on, the nights will grow longer and longer. Therefore, it can be said that Ragana is the goddess who keeps the world in balance between light and darkness, between birth and death. What would happen if the sun's force was left unchecked, and after the summer solstice its power only became stronger? The unbridled life force of the sun, if it continued simply to grow and grow, would bring disaster. It is thanks to Ragana that plants wither and people die so that a new life can come after them. This is worth remembering in today's overpopulated, overcrowded world, where the balance represented by Ragana is sadly lacking and all things appear to function in accordance with

Edward Abbey's remark: "Growth for the sake of growth alone is the ideology of the cancer cell."[35] As with Ragana at the summer solstice, it is another Underworld deity, Velnias, who battles to bring back the power of Saulė at the winter solstice. Even Ragana's negative powers may be understood as a blessing, and the heavenly world of sky remains in a state of perfect balance with the dark precincts of the Underworld. The starry crown of the World Tree is linked with its gnarled roots in the endless cycles of energy which make up the world.

After the advent of Christianity, Ragana was perceived simply as a witch who brought misfortune to humans and animals. Folk tales portrayed her as grotesque, like her Slavic counterpart Baba Yaga. She was seen as an evil enchantress who cast malicious spells upon human beings. But those who still remembered could still sing to her:

Ragana roams in summer fields,
Full of sunshine, bathed in gold.
Ragana roams in winter fields,
Dead in the silver time of night.
Ragana walked with me today.
Something was given,
And something was taken away.[36]

Ragana's special tree is the birch, the first one to begin blossoming and prophecy the coming spring.

Magical Working

To honor Ragana, give her the first eggs of spring as well as butter, cheese, hair, sheep's wool, and menstrual blood.

Five

Nature Spirits

THE LAUMĖS

Of all the goddesses and gods worshiped in the Baltic, the female Lithuanian spirits called Laumės may have been the oldest of them all, more ancient still than even the Mothers of the Neolithic, for the Laumės give some evidence of having originated in the period called the Mesolithic, just after the end of the Ice Age, when Europe was becoming thickly forested once again. While most Baltic deities are in human form—Perkūnas a sturdy fellow with a beard, Saulė a beautiful woman who loves to dance—the Laumės are still linked with the world of the animals. They had the claws of birds rather than the feet of human beings, the bodies of mortal women but sometimes the heads of goats. Other stories claim that they were half human and half dog, or, like the Greek centaurs, half horse. Often, they are said to have had only one eye. They were able to change themselves into animals altogether, usually mares, goats, bears, or dogs.

They lived in the sky and could be considered as atmospheric spirits. Laumės descended from the sky to Earth. They lived near lakes, abandoned bath-houses, on lake islands, or in the tangled wood of dense forests. Many water pools in Lithuania have names that are derived from the word Laumė. Laumės were afraid of tools made from iron, as were many spirits who dated from an era before the invention of metallurgy.

Laumės sometimes appeared as beautiful women, often naked or wearing very fine clothing, and in such a guise they were dangerous to men. Attracting their attention seductively, they would then tickle or tweak men to death and feast upon their bodies. Laumės liked to gather near rivers, lakes, swamps, or in meadows where dew fell in the night during the new moon or full moon. They danced and enjoyed themselves, leaving circles like fairy rings in the grass. Usually, Laumės were most powerful on a Friday (the day of Venus, the Love Goddess) during the new moon, or on the rainiest days of the month. Laumės could cause hail, storm, or rain by singing, dancing, or by casting spells. There was a Laumės song which was traditionally performed during weddings up until the nineteenth century. The song was performed by girls dancing in a circle, with one in the middle. This dance and song was also said to cause rain.

Rainbows were believed to be a ribbon lost by the Laumės, for they were said to be associated with weaving. They were able to do domestic work perfectly and were especially skilled in weaving and spinning. Laumės usually appeared in groups of three.

Though the Laumės were most often spoken of in the plural, sometimes the myths and legends speak of Laumė in the singular. In such stories, Laumė is said to be a beautiful goddess who lived in the clouds and had a diamond throne. Some legends assert that this goddess, Laumė, was the wife of the thunder god Perkūnas. Many tales, however, claim that they did not marry because Laumė fell in love with the Moon God, who, as we have seen, was quite a mischief-maker with the ladies. In other stories, she is stolen from Perkūnas by Velnias; as we have seen, this Lord of the Underworld was always the Thunder God's worst enemy. Velnias taught Laumė how to enjoy moonshine.

In yet another story, the bride of Perkūnas was a Laumė called Vaiva. The rainbow was called the ribbon of Vaiva. Despite her marriage, she fell in love with a singer named Straublys, and it was he who stole Vaiva's ribbon, the rainbow. During the rain, Straublys stretches the ribbon of Vaiva across the sky, which makes Perkūnas angry and causes him to shout with thunder. Therefore it was believed that it was the rainbow that caused the rain

Another myth claimed that Laumė, dwelling high in the atmosphere, fell in love with a beautiful young man who lived down on earth. They had a son named Meilius (a name which is derived from the word *meilė*, meaning "love," as is the name Milda). Laumė descended to the sky to breastfeed her son from time to time. However, Dievas found out about this son of sacrilegious love and tossed him into the highest part of the sky, thus giving him a place among the stars.

In Latvian mythology, Lauma is also singular rather than plural. She acts as an assistant at birth, ensuring the health and welfare of both mother and child. If the mother does not survive or gives the child up, she takes on the role of spiritual foster mother to the child. She spins the cloth of life for the child but weeps at the fate of some. The fact that the cloth can, to a degree, weave itself, indicates a higher power than Lauma, perhaps Laima or Māras.

Over the years, she became perceived as an evil old hag rather than a beautiful young woman. She weeps at her unfortunate fate, hoping for the day when people will once again see her as her former beautiful self.

Although Laumės can be dangerous, even fatal, to young and vital men, they love children. They also respect those who work hard and render help to those in need. They punish those who ridicule them, and those who are lazy (not unlike masquers we shall meet later on, who made unannounced visits to people's houses and vigorously spanked housewives and daughters who showed no industriousness or desire to work). Here is a folk tale featuring Laumės which bears a strong resemblance to the story of Mother Hulda as found in the tales of the Brothers Grimm:

A woman was harvesting a flower bed. She had taken her child with her and set the baby down in his bassinet while she worked, but she was so busy that the child slept all the day through, and she forgetfully left the little one behind.

The woman went home at the end of the day to milk the cows and make dinner. She served her husband, who asked her, "Where's my son?" With terror, she whispered, "I have forgotten him!" She ran as fast as she could to the place in which she left her son, and she heard a Laumė speak: "You have forgotten your child." The mother, thoroughly stricken now, asked the Laumė for her child back. The spirit said, "Come, dear woman, and take your child, for we have done nothing to him. We know that you work very hard at many jobs and that you did not intend to leave your child behind."

The fairies then went on to shower the baby with much treasure. The mother went home with her precious son and with her gifts; she was greeted by her husband with great joy.

Another woman, hearing of her good fortune, was overwhelmed with jealousy. She took to thinking, "I shall do the same as her, and I too shall be showered in gifts." The next evening, at dusk, she took her child, left him in the fields, and then went home. She ate dinner quite thoughtlessly before pausing to think of her child—and the treasure she hoped to obtain.

When she approached the field, hoping to find a pile of riches, she heard the fairies cry, "You left your child in greed!" And the child screamed with great pain, for he was pinched and tortured mercilessly, then thrown dead at the mother's feet.

The Laumės could be a dangerous and merciless collection of fairy folk indeed.

THE AITVARAS

An *aitvaras* is a nature spirit in Lithuanian mythology and is identical to the Latvian *pūķis*. An aitvaras is said to hatch from the egg of a 9- to 15-year-old rooster and looks like a white or black rooster with a fiery tail like a meteor.

In many cases, this Lithuanian creature is described as a household spirit which has the appearance of a bird when it is indoors—typically a black, golden, or white rooster with a fiery tail, as noted above. And yet it takes on the appearance of a dragon when it ventures outdoors.

An aitvaras will lodge itself in a house and most often refuse to leave. It brings both good and bad luck to the inhabitants of the house, for it provides its adopted home with stolen gold and grain, which can get the household into serious trouble if the theft is discovered.

An aitvaras can manifest itself as a flying ball of fire. In the Pagan Baltic, meteorites were often believed to be an aitvaras either in search of some treasure or on its way back to deliver it to their masters.

And the most gorgeous and poignant detail ever?

When an aitvaras dies, it becomes a spark.

In Latvia, this spirit is known as a pūķis, though Latvians do not regard their household dragons as particularly divine in nature.

Instead, they saw the pūķis as not very intelligent. When a pūķis attaches itself to a household, the family must take care of it. The pūķis always received the first bit of every meal. According to one account, if they felt they were not sufficiently revered and appreciated, they'd turn on their master and burn the house down. A pūķis was always kept hidden. Since no one but its master was allowed to lay eyes upon it, it was kept in a separate room with a sturdy lock. If the wrong person walked in and saw it, it would flee, and the bereaved master would have to go back to finding or making his own riches.

Like the Lithuanian aitvaras, the pūķis was also associated with the appearance of meteors.

THE LIETUVĒNS

There are some who, if they are hard-working, industrious, and love children, may not mind having a Laumė around the farm.

And there are some who, if they don't mind risking the wrath of their neighbors in order to acquire material goods, may find an aitvaras to be quite useful.

But no one wants a Lietuvēns.

Though the Lietuvēns, who is unique to Latvia, may somewhat resemble the Lithuanian Laumės, it is in other ways quite different, and much, much darker. In Latvian folklore, a Lietuvēns is the soul of a murdered person—usually hanged, strangled, or drowned—who is cursed to live in this world as long as it has been meant to live. Other sources say that a Lietuvēns is the soul of an unbaptized child. It is a malicious spirit that attacks both people and domestic animals. The condition known as sleep paralysis was said to be the result of someone being attacked by a Lietuvēns.

It is said that the Lietuvēns can find a way to get into your house, even by slipping through a keyhole. Not only can it cause nightmares, it can also strangle you.

The Lietuvēns is often described as a wretched-looking, miserable child. (This is clearly related to the stories which assert that the Lietuvēns is the soul of an unbaptized child.) It is small in height, moves very rapidly, and most often appears at noon or night. It can also take on the appearance of an ugly vicious woman. The Lietuvēns always leaves by way of the same place where it entered the house. While this may be a keyhole, it can also be a hole or crack in the wall, or perhaps a slot in the door.

The Lietuvēns rides and strangles sleeping people or domestic animals (often horses or cows). The victim quickly becomes weary, loses strength, and is covered in sweat because of the torturous experiences it undergoes. The weakened victim can see only a bit of the Lietuvēns, which feels as if it is lying on top of one with all its weight, preventing the sufferer from moving or running away. It becomes harder to breathe. In time, the Lietuvēns usually departs, leaving the victim on the verge of death rather than killing them outright.

Oddly enough, it was often said that the Lietuvēns doesn't torture animals and people who were born in the daytime.

According to folk traditions, there are some methods to get rid of a Lietuvēns. The hole, crack, or keyhole which serves as the entrance point for the Lietuvēns must be fixed with a piece of mottled wood. It should be cut with the left hand and brought to the house with the thick part first. All these things must be done at night after the Lietuvēns has already entered the house. If the Lietuvēns cannot find an exit, it may turn into a beautiful young woman and stay in the house while the exit is closed! But as soon as the point of entry is open again, it will escape immediately.

Another method of defense is that when under attack, a person must move the small or big toe of the left foot to get rid of the Lietuvēns. It will run away instantly.

Farm animals can be protected from a Lietuvēns with a knife, comb, or scythe attached to their back. In that case, the Lietuvēns will be hurt by the blades or sharp objects. The creature also might be caught in a moment of confusion, but it may only be attacked behind the animal's left ear. In that moment, it is suggested to hit it with a rowan stick so it will run away and won't come back. It is difficult for a Lietuvēns to strike at the animal if its back is oiled. It will be greasy, so the Lietuvēns won't be able to ride it. Another peculiar detail is that it is said that the Lietuvēns will try to avoid animals with a cut right ear.

If one can find the mortal bones of the Lietuvēns and bury them in a cemetery with proper honors, its tormented soul with never bother anyone else again. It is said that at the moment of such a burial, a thunderstorm will rise and lightning will strike, which means the poor lost soul has been properly taken to the Otherworld.

Magical Working

When one is dealing with a Lietuvēns, protective magic is called for. In addition to the methods already mentioned, there is the *Lietuvēns'* Cross, which is said to be the most effective of all.

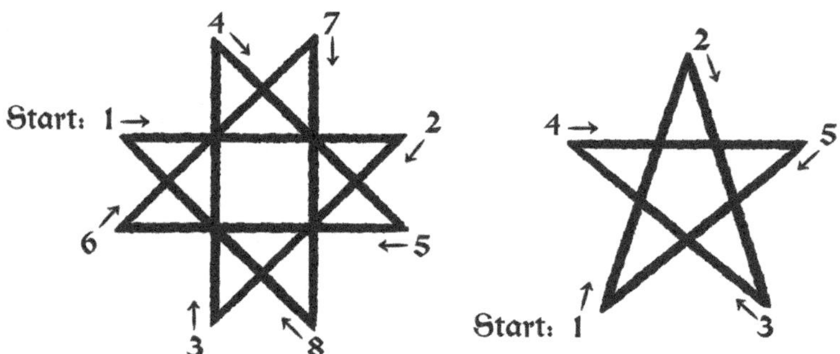

While the simplest form of the cross is a pentagram, the more complex version, shown here, is said to be more powerful. Such crosses could often be seen on doors, thresholds, windows, and other things. It can also be drawn on the hooves of cows and horses, and even people (especially on fingernails and toenails).

Part III: Lovers and Heroes

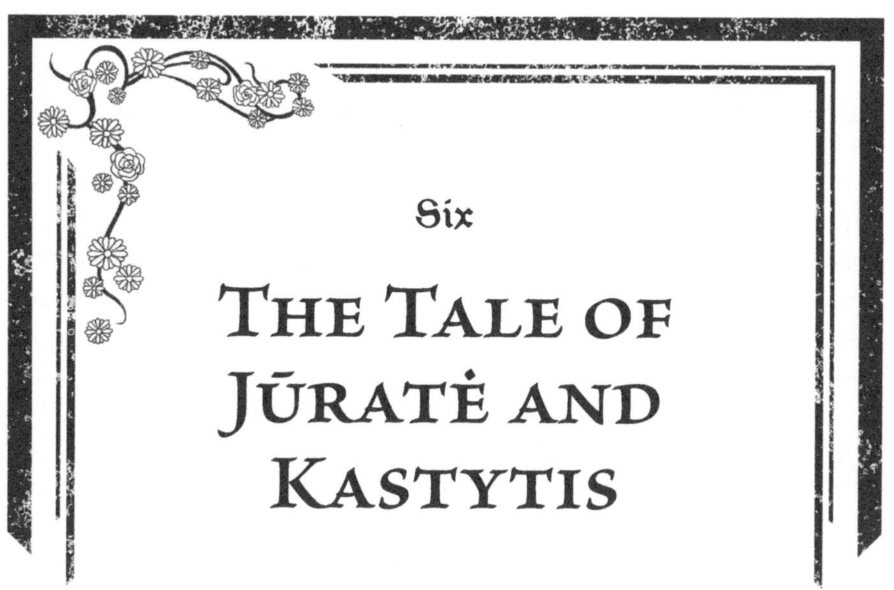

Six

The Tale of Jūratė and Kastytis

Once there was a castle, beneath the winding sea. It was a castle made of amber, shining brilliantly even beneath the darkness of the ocean. In the castle lived a maiden, a water nymph, in fact, a Goddess of the Waters, and her name was Jūratė, for the word *jūra* means "ocean," and Jūratė was the Goddess of the Sea.

Sometimes she looked out, with her magical vision, to enjoy the sights above—the boats, the birds, the wind, and the waves. And one day, she saw a young fisherman working in his boat, and his name was Kastytis, and he seemed very beautiful to her, so she called him to her, to live with her and love her in her amber castle underneath the sea. And they had great joy with each other.

But Perkūnas the Thunder God, gazing down upon the earth from his home in the sky, looked down into the world beneath the waves, and he saw something which he, as a guardian of Cosmic Law, believed to be terribly, terribly wrong—an immortal goddess and a mortal man, bound together as lovers.

In fury, Perkūnas cast a thunderbolt so powerful that it ripped its way through sky and forest and farther still, to the world beneath the sea, where it struck Jūratė's castle, and shattered its amber beauty into pieces.

Kastytis tried to escape. He was swimming for his life. But it was all to no avail. The Thunder God raised a storm, and Jūratė's lover sank, helplessly, into the sea and drowned.

She mourns for him to this very day. She weeps tears of amber. Along with the shattered pieces of her castle, her tears floated to the shore, and this is why the Baltic coast is rich in amber.

The tale of Jūratė and Kastytis appeared in print for the first time in 1842, in the writings of Liudvikas Adomas Jucevičius. In 1920, Maironis, one of Lithuania's best-known poets, wrote a ballad to honor the lovers, and much of the legend's present popularity is due to this ballad.

Even in a region as cold and northerly as Lithuania, people still enjoy the beach, and Palanga, the most popular beach resort in the nation, has a monument dedicated to Jūratė and Kastytis. It is located in a square right next to a bridge that leads into the sunset—a very popular tourist attraction. The Palanga coat of arms was designed with the legend of Jūratė and Kastytis in mind, featuring the silver crown and the amber tears of the goddess Jūratė.

Jūratė and Kastytis continue to appear in the arts in Lithuania. In 1955 the composer Kazimieras Viktoras Banaitis finished an opera but was forced into exile because of his resistance to the Communist regime, and his work was not produced until 1972 in Chicago. In a more contemporary vein, a rock opera based on the legend was performed in the Lithuanian city of Klaipeda in 2002.

Seven

Eglė, the Queen of Serpents

There are some stories which are found throughout the world with such remarkable similarities that scholars recognize them as having been derived from a single source. How, then—setting aside, for the moment, speculations about lost continents or loquacious aliens—can one explain such a phenomenon?

Joseph Campbell, a scholar of world mythology, suggested that such tales all have their origin in shamanism.[37] They most likely developed in Siberia, before our ancient ancestors began the long, long walks which led them west to the European continent and east into the western hemisphere. For example, the Italian historian Carlo Ginzburg has demonstrated that the fairytale we call Cinderella is worldwide and originated in the story of a young woman's encounter with the old shamanic Bone Goddess, the initiator.[38]

The story of the woman who becomes Queen of the Serpents is likewise a story told throughout the world, although the most elaborate versions are to be found in the Baltic. No one can even hazard a guess at how old it really is. While I shall not venture to record variations from South and Central Asia or other parts of Europe, nor will I address the Native American versions, I will give a fair number of Baltic variants if only to demonstrate the richness of the human mind in weaving variations upon a common theme, stories within a story, the magic of the imagination.

The Lithuanian version of the story in its classic form first appeared in print in 1837, published by one M. Jasevičiaus or M. Jasavičius, in the supplement *Biruta.* Biruta, or more properly *Birutė,* is a name which shall occupy us later on in yet another unusual dimension of mythology.

Eglė, the Queen of Serpents is one of the best-known Lithuanian folk tales. *Ĕglė* is a noun meaning the tree species spruce (Latin: *Picea*) and fir, with cognates in other Baltic languages: Latvian *egle,* "spruce, fir," and Old Prussian *addle,* "spruce, fir."

The story features not only human-reptile shapeshifting but human-tree shapeshifting as well. Numerology is also evident in the tale, such as twelve sons, three daughters, three days, three tricks, three weeks of feasting, nine years under the oath of marriage, the three tasks given to Eglė by her husband to fulfill, and nine days of visits.

As noted above, the most elaborate versions of this global myth are to be found in the Baltic, which even has certain place-names that appear to be related to this story. I am not claiming that there was any sort of historical event in the Baltic region which served as the origin of the tale; these toponyms or place-names simply testify to the story's importance in that region and suggest that Baltic peoples believed that these place-names marked the area where the mythic tale took place. There is a sector of the Baltic coast where Poland, Lithuania, and a detached piece of Russia all come together. Neopagan Lithuanians have always held that this is a region of great importance and was the location of Romuva, the great shrine of the World Tree discussed in Chapter One. In fact, the Neopagan Lithuanian community planted a tree named Romuva in the Russian city of Kaliningrad, which also lies in the area. In what is now northeastern Poland, there is a region called Augustów where two places, a lake named Jeglówek and a village named Jegliniec, are located. Jegle is the Polish name which corresponds to Eglė, and the area was formerly inhabited by a tribe known as the Yotvingians, who had a fortress in what is now Jegliniec. Unfortunately, the Teutonic Knights succeeded in waging a campaign of complete genocide against the Yotvingians, and there are none of them left. We are not clear on whether they were more closely associated with the Old Prussians or Lithuanians, although most scholars would argue in favor of the latter.

Earlier in the present volume, we had spoken of the žaltys, a peaceful grass snake which served as a household spirit in Pagan Lithuania. As the sacred animal of the sun goddess Saulė, the žaltys was regarded as a guardian of the home and a symbol of fertility. People kept it as a pet by the stove or some other special area of the house. It was said to bring good harvest and wealth, whereas killing a žaltys was said to bring great misfortune upon a household. If a žaltys was found in the field, people gave it milk, attempting to coax the creature into the house, take up residence in the warmth behind the stove, and become the sacred household pet.

Once, in times long ago, a young maiden named Eglė discovered a žaltys in the sleeve of her blouse after she had been bathing in the local lake (Jeglówek?) with her two sisters. Speaking in a human voice, the žaltys repeatedly agreed to crawl away and return Eglė's clothes to her only after she pledged herself to him in marriage. Eglė was not only dismayed, she was shocked, for one species cannot truly marry another. Just as incest represents a union which is too close, marriage with animals represents a union which is too distant. The same motif can be seen in the stories of men who marry—always unsuccessfully in the long run—with swan maidens, or in tales of a woman's marriage to the Great Silkie of Sule Skerrie.

To get rid of the annoying reptile, Eglė agreed to marry him. Deep inside, she regarded the whole matter as rather silly, despite the fact that the snake had spoken in a human voice, and clearly, there was magic afoot.

Eglė failed to understand the seriousness of the situation. After three days, thousands of grass snakes came slithering into the yard of her parents' house (in Jegliniec?). They had come to claim Eglė as their master's bride and their future queen.

Her family tried to trick the multitude of serpents. First, they brought forth a goose and said that this was Eglė. But as they began their journey home, with the goose in their midst, a cuckoo—which, as we have seen, was regarded as a prophetic bird—warned them from its perch in a birch tree that this was not Eglė but just a bird.

Angrily, the snakes returned to the farmhouse and demanded the genuine article. Again Eglė's family tried to trick them and gave them a sheep. Once again, the prophetic cuckoo cried out in warning. The snakes returned, somewhat angrier this time. Baffled and now a bit frightened, Eglė's family gave them a cow. Again the cuckoo cried out against the deceit. This time, the snakes were truly infuriated. Being magical animals who could bestow either prosperity or misfortune upon a household, they threatened to curse the entire village with a dry year of no rain followed by a destructive deluge and, ultimately, famine throughout the village. This time the family surrendered and gave up Eglė to the snakes, who first took her to a lagoon at the shore of the sea and then beneath it to where their king, who had hidden himself in Eglė's clothing, was waiting for his bride.

The žaltys king was named Žilvinas, and he transformed himself into a handsome young man in order to greet his bride Eglė. He took her from the lagoon to a nearby island (there is an island in Lake Jeglówek), and from there to his true home beneath the sea, to his beautiful palace. Some versions of the story claim that the Serpent King wears an amber crown or that he lived in an amber palace—a motif that recalls the tale of Jūratė and Kastytis. Eglė, now immortal, will dwell beneath the sea for the rest of eternity. The marriage feast lasted for three weeks, and the couple lived quite happily together. In fact, Eglė bore four children to the Serpent King. Her three sons were called Ąžuolas (Oak), Uosis (Ash), and Beržas (Birch), and her youngest child was a daughter who was called Drebulė (Aspen). Eglė almost forgot about her homeland, but then one day, after nine years of marriage, her oldest son Ąžuolas questioned her about her parents, and she decided to pay a visit to her former home. But Žilvinas possessed magical intuition, and he knew that if Eglė left, she would never return, so he strictly forbade her to go and visit her human family unless she fulfilled three seemingly impossible tasks: to spin a never-ending tuft of silk, to wear down a pair of iron shoes, and to bake a pie with no utensils.

Eglė managed to make contact with a sorceress who seems, from a mythological perspective, to have been the Lady of the Sea or the Lady of the Cave, and she succeeded in accomplishing her tasks. Žilvinas reluctantly allowed Eglė to go home and take her children with her to visit their human grandparents. Prior to their departure, however, he told his children the secret of how to magically call him from the depths of the sea and instructed them not to tell the secret to anyone else.

After the return of the long-lost family member Eglė, her relatives did not wish to let her return to the sea. They decided to try and kill Žilvinas, despite the fact that he was apparently an immortal as well as a sacred žaltys. First, his sons were threatened and beaten with the scourge by their uncles in an effort to make them reveal the magic words that would summon their father; however, they remained silent and did not betray him. Finally, the young daughter Aspen became frightened and spoke the magic words:

Žilvinas, dear Žilvinėlis,
If you're alive—may the sea foam milk.
If you're dead—may the sea foam blood.

Eglė had twelve brothers, and they sent forth the magic call to Žilvinas. When he emerged from the sea in order to respond to the summons that he believed to have come from his children, they used scythes to kill him. They said nothing to their sister about the crime they had committed.

While the killing of Žilvinas by Eglė's brothers may seem like a heinous and somewhat unmotivated crime, in the Pagan metaphysics of the Baltic it is also a restoration of cosmic order. The snake is the ruler of the waters, and thus he represents a primal, chaotic world. His liaison with Eglė, and the birth of their half-human, half-reptilian children, not only violates the boundaries between the world of land and the world of water, but the world of humans and the world of animals. By killing the snake, it could be said that the brothers restore the natural order of things. As we shall see, Eglė had a different opinion.

After nine days, Eglė returned to the seashore and called her husband, but only foaming blood washed up from the sea. Then Eglė heard the voice of her dead husband's spirit and discovered how he had died. This too is an important mythic statement about the natural order of things, for by using the magical incantation to summon Žilvinas, Eglė builds a bridge between the human world and the chthonic, underground realm.

Eglė became angry and cast a spell which turned her fearful daughter into her namesake, an aspen tree—and this is why the aspen quakes as if in fear. (In other versions of the story, her name is Willow, and this is why the willow weeps.) But as we have seen, the Baltic peoples and their Slavic neighbors had a strong reverence for trees, and to be reincarnated as a tree was considered a great honor. Having already broken the boundaries between earth and sea, this world and the Otherworld, and the boundaries between humans and animals, Eglė took yet another step and broke another boundary—that between the human kingdom and the plant kingdom. After transforming her daughter into an aspen (or willow), she turned her sons into strong, beautiful, majestic trees—an oak, an ash, and a birch. And at last, in a final farewell to the world of humans and animals, Eglė transformed herself into a spruce—or, according to some versions of the story, into a fir, which is a similar tree from the same family.

In eastern Lithuania, Eglė's children are more often said to have the names of birds rather than trees, and it is birds into which they are transformed.

In Latvian versions of the tale, the young woman's husband is sometimes killed by her brothers, as in the Lithuanian version, but in other stories, her life as the Sea King's wife and her transformation from the human world into the animal world is successfully accomplished.

In a Polish tale which has been translated as *Jegle and the King of the Lakes* and which may have Old Prussian origins, a fisherman had two sons and went to fish in a nearby lake (again, Lake Jeglówek may be the location intended), when suddenly, a storm began to rage. The lake grew turbulent, threatening to drown the man. However, he was rescued by a mysterious man with greenish hair who introduces himself as Zaltis, the King of the Lakes. The fisherman was very thankful for the rescue and asked what he could offer in return; Zaltis said that he wanted the fisherman's most valuable possession, and promised to grant him an abundance of fish for his whole life.

The fisherman returned home and discovered that his wife had given birth to a baby girl whom they named Jegle. Years passed, the fisherman's wife died, and Jegle managed the household whenever her father and brothers were away. She liked to spend her days dipping her feet in the water, and a large green fish played between her feet.

Later, an old woman paid a visit to Jegle and told her that she brought news from Jegle's bridegroom, Zaltis, and told the girl to meet him by the edge of the lake the following day. Jegle went to the lake to meet Zaltis, who was in human form, and he took her to his underwater palace. They lived happily for a time, until the day that Jegle began to miss her father and longed to visit him. Zaltis agreed to let her visit him, and he took her to the world above the lake. Jegle was happy to visit her father, but her brothers secretly decided to win her back from the King of the Lakes. After her visit, Jegle returned to the edge of the lake to wait for her husband; her brothers followed her and waited for Zaltis to emerge from the lake. As soon as the king surfaced, Jegle's brothers tried to grab him, but his magic turned them into stones. Zaltis took Jegle back to their palace and explained that her brothers would be restored to human form after a while.

So here again, in a version which may have Old Prussian origins and which may well have originated in the region which still bears names associated with the myth, the young woman's bridge between the world of humans and of animals remains secure.

In versions of the story from nearby Russia, the Serpent King or King of the Lake is almost always murdered, and the young woman is sometimes named Masha.

Part IV: The Wheel of Life

Eight

The Baltic Calendar

Though Pagan texts may exist—the Homeric and Orphic hymns, the Norse Eddas and skaldic poems, the sagas and stories of the Celtic lands—they are not "holy scriptures." They do not propound rules that must be obeyed in order to avoid what the monotheistic religions perceive as "damnation." Any Pagan faith is based upon the shared life experience of one's ancestors, as well as one's community and one's own personal experience. The Greek hymns and Norse tales, the *Mabinogion*, and the Welsh Triads are all part of that shared life experience, and it is the experience that is sacred, not the text. Baltic Paganism, whose primary texts are whimsical folk songs, exemplifies the same principles. It is not the words of a song which are sacred; it is the life experiences of all the songmakers over countless generations which is sacred.

The Baltic lands were the last bastions of European Paganism. Even after the "official" conversion of Grand Duke Vytautas of Lithuania in 1386—a blatantly political maneuver which fooled absolutely no one—the ancient religious rites continued to be practiced, much to the chagrin of the unsuccessful missionaries whom Vytautas and his successors allowed to enter their lands (and who were more or less ignored by the ruling class, which had more important things to do). Lithuania remained essentially Pagan until the eighteenth century. Cults both communal and individual continued to be practiced into the nineteenth and even the twentieth century. Even communism had little impact upon them. When the Baltic lands were released from Soviet hegemony in 1989, Neopagan organizations quickly sprouted up in both Lithuania and Latvia.

The names of the goddesses and gods had never been forgotten. The people had never stopped singing the *dainas* and *dainos* which commemorated the actions of their Pagan deities. There were literally hundreds of divine beings—a goddess of the forest, a goddess of bees, and, of course, a god of beer! In approaching them, there are a few things that it is good to remember, and which are acknowledged by most Baltic Neopagans today.

Firstly, the world is a living thing, and like all living things, it deserves our respect, even our love. When we pay homage to the goddesses and gods of rain and thunder, fire and water, bees and beer, and sex and death, we worship the world with love and respect.

Second, we must remember that the world is harmonious, that there is harmony in all things. But harmony is never constant. The seasons grow and die, and so do we. Things fall out of harmony and must be put back together again. The cycle of life and death, of growth and decay, must go on—an orderly, harmonious, flowing, moving cosmos.

The gods create the flow of harmony in the world. This is especially true of the high gods and goddesses—Dievas the creator; Perkūnas the thunder god, rainmaker, protector of the cosmic order; Žemyna the Earth Mother, who is present in every rock and in the music of every stream, in every plant and every tree; Laima, who weaves our fate and the fate of all other living things as well; and Saulė, the bright and shining sun, who weeps red tears that turn to berries, and who joins us at the summer solstice time to dance and sing.

The two most important cycles concern Saulė herself. Her strength grows throughout the spring; such is the world's harmony, that the sun may increase in the springtime. But by the summer solstice, harmony can only be maintained if her growth is controlled and turned back; otherwise, plants and trees would proliferate to the point where they overwhelm all else. It is Ragana the Witch Goddess who maintains the harmony of the world by turning Saulė back at the solstice, sending her down a different path, a path of waning light that maintains the balance of the world. But by the time of the winter solstice, her light is so dim that forces of darkness might well take control if it were not for the Underworld Lord and his army of the dead, our ancestors, who battle against the dark on the winter solstice until Saulė's light returns.

But the gods need our help to maintain the world's harmony, and that is what worshiping them is all about. We give them strength, and they give us life. It is human nature to seek harmony, to protect it, and maintain it. Thus, the harmonious balance of the world and its cycles is the foundation of Pagan faith and our worship of the goddesses and gods. For indeed, these deities may be invisible to our eyes, but to Pagan believers, they are as eminently real as we ourselves. They may thrive in certain sacred places or show themselves as actors in the course of human events. The gods are Nature itself.

In order to assist the cosmos in maintaining its balance and harmony, we must try to live on the path of rightness, a path which, in Baltic Paganism, is established by Dievas, the creator. And it is a part of our path to celebrate the festivals which mark the ebb and flow of harmony and the maintenance of cosmic balance.

Because we all share in the celebration of the festivals, we all share in sustaining the harmony of the world. In that respect, Paganism is a communal endeavor. All of us play our role, our part in the cosmic game. Paganism is not a religion that is "preached." There are no "official" sacred texts because they are not needed. Paganism is simply lived. The monotheistic religions are packed with individuals who feel compelled to "preach" the religion. Christianity, for example, has its St. Paul and its St. Jerome, and it has those who rebelled against them, its Jan Hus and its Martin Luther. A traditional way of life needs no preachers. When it is time to light the fires, the village gathers, and the fires are lit. When it is time to dance around the sacred tree, the villagers gather by the sacred tree. Only in its final days, when it was attacked by Christianity, did Paganism produce "teachers" who felt compelled to "preach" the Pagan way, and there were only a few of them—Iamblichus, the Emperor Julian, Hypatia of Alexandria. The harvest needs no preachers, only harvesters—and, of course, the sacredness of the earth, whose cycles of harmony and balance are maintained by one and all.

Our ancestors too are part of the sacredness of the earth. Gods they may not be, but they too work to maintain the harmony of the world. They emerge from the Underworld to visit us, to give us their wisdom, and upon the winter solstice, they join in the fight to bring Saulė back into the light. Therefore, we must remember them and honor them just as we honor the goddesses and gods. The ancient rites which go by the rather dismissive term of "ancestor worship" were created for this kind of remembrance. Just as the gods are Nature, so are the dead, for death is the most natural thing that there is. As we have seen in the previous chapters, the Baltic peoples believed that our ancestors may be with us in the nearest tree, in the flight of a butterfly, as well as in the girl down the street. The living and the dead never cease to encounter each other.

In the final analysis, it is simple: The gods are Nature and Nature is holy. All of us are educated by Nature and her cycles, her dance of harmony. Nature is our ultimate teacher. And our calendars chart the dance of Nature's cycles.

We all know what time is—or think we do. It is a succession of dawns and sunsets, days and nights, and seasons. We may divide it into hours and minutes or years and centuries, but we can never step outside of it—except perhaps in moments of special awareness which constitute the peak experiences of life. Time is one of the essential words. Time is an inescapable fact of existence. We as a species have always been inclined to regard time as a kind of taskmaster, a relentless clock that holds us always in its grasp, ticking away the minutes toward our eventual extinction. Time is the linear reality that gives shape and pattern to our lives, defining our mortality.

According to many traditional societies, there are two dimensions of time: ordinary time and sacred time.

What has just been described is ordinary time.

If ordinary time represents a process to which all of us are subject and before which all of us are ultimately powerless, then sacred time represents cosmic order. It is the foundation of rhythm and motion. It is the glue that binds the universe together. Without the sense of cosmic order implied by this sacred dimension of time, nothing could happen. There would be no loom upon which to weave the tapestry of life. In many ancient mythologies, the gods do their work of universal creation in a world where time does not yet exist. Time itself is the summit of creation, for it is only when time exists that the new-made world is ready for humankind. The creation of time replaces original chaos with cosmic order. Marduk, king of the gods of ancient Babylon, slays the primordial serpent Tiamat, symbolic of chaos, and when he is done he "sets the stars in their courses" and thus establishes the calendar. Similarly, the Viking god Odin and his brothers slay the great frost-giant Ymir, fashioning the world from his carcass and, finally, attending to the calendar by putting the heavens in order.

Sacred time exists contemporaneously with ordinary time. It is fashioned of the same elements—seasonal and celestial—which comprise ordinary time. It is simply our altered or ritualized perception of time that allows us to enter its sacred dimension.

We enter ritual space in our daily lives whenever we pray or meditate, whenever we create—in short, whenever we pay homage to the presence of the divine in our lives. For that moment, we are at the center of the universe. Whenever we enter ritual space, we enter ritual time as well. Ordinary time may be going on all around us, but we are no longer a part of it. Our perception of time has changed. It is no longer a mere progression of hours and minutes, but a living, vital, spiritual presence. This is what the sacred dimension of time is all about.

Thus humanity has devised rituals to mark the four major changes of the solar and seasonal year—the equinoxes, when day and night are of equal length, and the solstices, when the sun appears to stand still and then "turn back" to the north or south. Priests and magicians of all cultures have charted the progress of planets and fixed the positions of the stars, for the orderly cycles of the heavens are among the most potent symbols of the cosmic order—remember, Marduk and Odin created time by "setting the stars in their courses." Facing east, the yogi honors the rising of the sun each day, and so pays homage to the sun as a symbol of the Self; thus he enters into ritual time—which, paradoxically, is timeless, even as the Self is eternal.

However, an evolving world is a world in turmoil, and therefore it needs to be centered, equilibrated, and maintained so that it shall not fall out of balance. Human beings must constantly struggle for the sense of universal order and harmony even as they struggle towards their own evolution.

To pluck order out of chaos we must measure the ebb and flow of energy in time, the transformations and metamorphoses that make up life on earth. We must find the sense of cosmic order in this shifting, restless world of volcanic passions, both human and terrestrial.

And for this task, we have calendars.

The calendar of the Pagan Baltic is an extraordinarily complex system of ritual, magic, and mythology. Contemporary Neopagans from the Baltic lands have devoted a great deal of thought and speculation—some of it quite mathematical—to the intricacies of their ancient calendar.[39] To understand it, let us begin with the myth that it embodies. It is a myth which encompasses not only the birth, growth, death, and rebirth of the earth itself but also of all of us who live upon it, for we mortals too are subject, both psychologically and incarnationally, to the same eternal process.

THE SEASONS

In Pagan times, it was said that the four seasons corresponded with the four stages of human life. Easter was the time of childhood, while summer was the time of youth. Autumn corresponded to maturity, and winter to old age.

Winter

The ancient Baltic year turns upon the solstices and equinoxes, and these four days of the year spell the most significant changes in the cosmic cycle. The year begins upon the winter solstice, when Saulė, the sun, is at her weakest, and the world—frozen and gloomy with long nights and short days—seems as if dead. When Saulė is reborn at the darkest time of the year and begins to move back toward the north, toward brighter days and bright new harvests, the world itself is born again. In the phases of human life, winter corresponds to old age, when the life force is weakening. Death is near, but so is rebirth.

Spring

By the time spring begins at the vernal equinox, the earth is green enough for Žemyna, the Earth Goddess, who has been asleep beneath the ground while the world is frozen and cold, to emerge as a beautiful young woman, still untouched and virginal. In human life, the vernal equinox is our birth and our childhood, just as it is the Earth Mother's. A month after the equinox, around April 21 or 22, Žemyna will marry an aspect of Dievas who was called *Pergrūbris* by the Old Prussians and *Praamžis* in Lithuania. Though Praamžis is typically perceived as a white-bearded elder, an "old man god," he manifests himself as a young man for his wedding; the Prussians thought of him as riding to his wedding on a horse, like a young warrior but not bearing arms, for his mission is one of peace rather than war.

Summer

After the marriage of Mother Earth and Father Sky, sowing and planting can begin. The earth grows greener, and the crops grow taller until the summer solstice when the days are long, and the nights are short. As human beings, this is the time of youthful vigor, when the life force is strong within us, and all things seem possible. But if Saulė, who has nourished Žemyna with her celestial fire, were allowed to continue growing and growing, there would be dire consequences. With less night and longer, hotter days, the green world would proliferate to such a degree that it would overpower the delicate balance of the cycle of the year. First, there would be a profusion of plants and trees and crops, then Saulė herself, continuing to grow in power, would overwhelm the world with her light, and the trees, plants, and crops would wither and die from too much heat. Saulė, despite her loving, benevolent intentions, must be brought to a halt. This is the job of Ragana the Witch Goddess, who turns Saulė back on the summer solstice so that she travels to the south now rather than the north, the days growing shorter and the nights growing longer.

Autumn

As with the vernal equinox, another point of perfect balance is reached at the autumn equinox when the crops will be harvested. This season of abundance is joyful, rich, and extremely sexual. Afterward, the darkness will grow while the day is waning. Žemyna will begin to retreat beneath the earth for her winter sleep. The souls of the dead, our cherished ancestors, will emerge from the Underworld for their sojourn in our own world. And we, as mature human beings now, will have the wisdom to welcome them and understand them.

And indeed, the dead have their own role to play. Just as the forces of light, if left unchecked, would spin the world out of balance, the time has now come when the forces of darkness threaten to do the same. Saulė has weakened to the point where she provides but little light and the world is a dark, cold, and lonely place. Upon the winter solstice, Velnias, the God of the Underworld, will muster his army, the spirits of the dead, and he will lead them in battle against the dark forces. Velnias will win. The light of Saulė will return. The earth will slowly thaw, and in time, the day of equal balance, the vernal equinox, will return. The souls of the dead, having protected their descendants once again, will begin their journey back to the Underworld. Žemyna will re-awaken from her winter sleep, the virgin will become a wife, and Perkūnas will gift the world with his life-giving rain as Saulė grows bright again.

THE "TIMES" AND THEIR FESTIVALS

Each of the four seasons is comprised of three months or ninety days, from an equinox to a solstice or from a solstice to an equinox. Anyone who is familiar with the common Neopagan calendar, which is modeled on Celtic tradition, will know of the so-called "cross-quarter days" which fall directly in between the solstices and equinoxes and divide each season into two halves. To use their well-known Celtic names, these days, beginning from the winter solstice, are Imbolc, Beltane (May Day), Lughnasa, and Samhain (Halloween). Between the winter solstice and Imbolc, therefore, is a period of forty-five days, and then another forty-five days between Imbolc and the spring equinox.

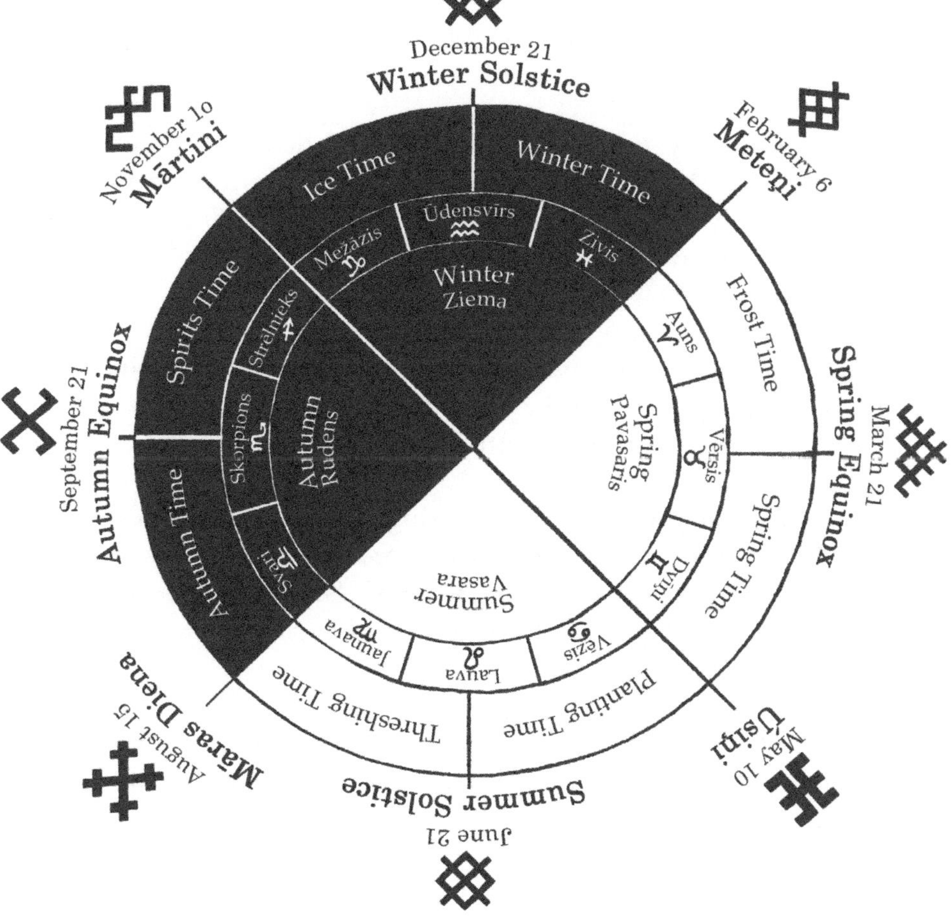

December 21
Winter Solstice
February 6
Meteņi
March 21
Spring Equinox
May 10
Ūsiņi
June 21
Summer Solstice
August 15
Māras Diena
September 21
Autumn Equinox
November 10
Mārtini
Ice Time
Winter Time
Frost Time
Spring Time
Planting Time
Threshing Time
Autumn Time
Spirits Time
Mežāzis
Ūdensvīrs
Zivis
Auns
Vērsis
Dvīņi
Vēzis
Lauva
Jaunava
Svari
Skorpions
Strēlnieks
Winter
Ziema
Spring
Pavasaris
Summer
Vasara
Autumn
Rudens

In Baltic Paganism, each of the "half seasons" or forty-five-day periods was treated as a separate unit of time and had its own name. The most detailed descriptions of these forty-five-day cycles come from Latvia, where each of these periods was called a *laiks* or "Time." At the end of each *laiks*, a special festival was held, just as in the Pagan Celtic lands. Here is a description of the Times, based upon the Latvian year:

The forty-five-day *laiks* after the winter solstice, or *Ziemassvētki*, corresponds to the first half of winter and was known as *Sala Laiks*, which basically means "Winter Time" (though that is not an exact translation), and it culminated in the festival of *Meteņi*, or "Throwing Away," which is equivalent to the Celtic Imbolc.

The forty-five-day period between Meteņi and the spring equinox, or *Lieldienas*, corresponds to the second half of winter and was called *Sērsnu Laiks* or "Frozen Ice-Crust Time."

The forty-five-day period after the spring equinox which corresponds to the first half of spring was known as *Sulu Laiks* or simply "Spring Time," and it culminated in the festival of Úsiņi, named in honor of a Pagan Baltic god who was the protector of horses. His festival time is equivalent to the Celtic Beltane.

The forty-five-day period between Úsiņi and the summer solstice, or Jāņi, corresponds to the second half of spring and was called *Sējas Laiks* or "Sowing Time."

The forty-five-day period after the summer solstice corresponds to the first half of summer and was known as *Siena Laiks* or "Haying Time." It culminated in the festival of Māras, held in honor of the goddess Māra, whom we met in an earlier chapter. It is equivalent to the Celtic Lughnasa.

The forty-five-day period between Māras and the autumn equinox, or Apjumības, corresponds to the second half of summer and was called *Rudzu Laiks* or "Rye Bread Time."

The forty-five-day period after the autumn equinox corresponds to the first half of fall and was known as *Veļu Laiks* or "Laundry Time," and it culminated in the festival of Mārtiņi, or Martin's Day. The somewhat mysterious use of the word "laundry" refers to the linen tablecloths set out at that time to honor the return of the ancestral spirits; Mārtiņi is therefore equivalent to the Celtic Samhain.

The forty-five-day period between Mārtiņi and the winter solstice corresponds to the second half of fall and was known as *Ledus Laiks* or "Time of Ice."

The cycle of Times can easily be laid out in table form:

Winter	Winter Time (Sala Laiks) Winter Solstice to Meteņi (December 21 to February 5–6) ———— ❂ ———— Frozen Ice-Crust Time (Sērsnu Laiks) Meteņi to Vernal Equinox (February 5–6 to March 21)
Spring	Spring Time (Sulu Laiks) Vernal Equinox to Úsiņi (March 21 to May 5–6) ———— ❂ ———— Spring Time (Sulu Laiks) Úsiņi to Summer Solstice (May 5–6 to June 21)
Summer	Haying Time (Siena Laiks) Summer Solstice to Māras (June 21 to August 5–6) ———— ❂ ———— Rye Bread Time (Rudzu Laiks) Māras to Autumnal Equinox (August 5–6 to September 21)
Autumn	"Laundry" Time (Veļu Laiks) Autumnal Equinox to Mārtiņi (September 21 to November 5–6) ———— ❂ ———— Time of Ice (Ledus Laiks) Mārtiņi to Winter Solstice (November 5–6 to December 21)

The attentive and/or astrologically experienced reader will notice that I have listed the festivals of the "cross-quarter" days not for the exact days upon which they were celebrated in Celtic tradition but for the days that usually mark the sun's position at fifteen degrees of the fixed signs of the zodiac, sometimes referred to as the "true" cross-quarter days, which are the ones most likely to mark an actual forty-five-day interval between solstices and equinoxes. This has been done for the sake of continuity and precision. Just as the Celtic holidays may commonly be celebrated a few days from the sun's exact position at the middle of fixed zodiacal signs, so it is with the Baltic countries as well. In fact, the dates during which many such "cross-quarter" holidays have been celebrated in Baltic lands have sometimes changed dramatically due to Christian influence. The same is true all over Europe. The summer solstice, when the sun reaches the first degree of the cardinal sign Cancer, typically falls between June 20 and 22, with June 21 being the most common. Yet when Shakespeare wrote *A Midsummer Night's Dream*, he was referring to June 23 rather than June 21. Why? Because June 24 was the Catholic feast day of St. John the Baptist, and Christian priests altered the date for celebrating Midsummer ceremonies to bring them into accordance with Christian theology.

The same process took place in the Baltic, with some festivals, notably Úsiņi and Māras, being changed quite dramatically—Úsiņi, which ought to have been celebrated on the May 5 or 6 and had a correspondence with the Celtic Beltane, was moved to April 23 to bring it into harmony with the Catholic ceremonies for St. George's day—in fact, even the name was changed to *Jūrgi*, the Baltic form of "George," and Māras was moved from early August to August 15 to match the Feast of the Assumption of St. Mary. But the precise dates of the forty-five-day "Times," with a bit of allowance for the Earth's perpetual "wobble" in its orbit, are as given here.

It will be noted that these forty-five "Times" all have a deep relationship with Nature. In order to truly obtain a deep inner sense or understanding of this Pagan Baltic calendar, we need to pay attention to the changes of the seasons. Many contemporary Neopagans live in climates and regions which are quite different from that of the Baltic, and in any case, many are urban dwellers, where the agricultural cycles upon which the "Times" are based have no relevance.

In order to gain a better understanding of the way in which these forty-five-day periods "worked," it is helpful to be aware of the seasonal changes around us, no matter in what climatic zone we may live. Too often, we walk past a magnificent tree without even looking up from our cell phones, unaware that we are in the presence of Laima, whose sacred tree is a linden, or Perkūnas, whose tree is the stately oak. We often think of rain as something which has spoiled our barbecue rather than seeing it as the action of Perkūnas upon the Earth Mother Žemyna. But whatever your weather may be like or however large the city in which you live, paying attention to the weather and the bits and pieces of Nature around you will help you to better understand the rituals we will soon describe.

THE OLD PRUSSIAN ZODIAC

The astrological twelve-sign zodiac was imported to the Baltic at some point—though we do not know at what point. An old chronicle tells us that a Lithuanian temple of the thirteenth century, dedicated to Perkūnas, contained twelve steps and that each month, a sacred flame was lit upon one of the steps. Archaeological excavations beneath the Cathedral of Vilnius confirm the truth of this assertion, though the names that the Lithuanians may have given to the zodiacal constellations have not survived.

A cup found near Grodno, in the former territory of the Old Prussians and now in the nation of Belarus, provides us with more detail. Not only is it illustrated with pictures of each zodiacal sign, the names are given in most cases, and we can see that the Old Prussians were not only aware of the zodiac, but that they thoroughly transformed it into something uniquely Baltic.[40]

Not only have the names of the zodiacal signs been changed to reflect Baltic cultural values, but some Neopagans of the Old Prussian tradition believe that a kind of yin-yang polarity, which one writer describes as an "antipodal" paradigm, has been imposed upon the zodiac so that the qualities attributed to the signs often match up with the opposite sign.[41] Though names and qualities for some of the zodiacal signs are sadly missing, a basic concept comes through:

> *In winter, the zodiacal signs take their names and qualities from the opposite or antipodal constellations to the position of the Sun.*
>
> *In spring, the signs of the zodiac take their names and qualities from the zodiacal constellations which the Sun occupies.*
>
> *In summer, the zodiacal signs take their names and qualities from the opposite or antipodal constellations to the position of the Sun.*
>
> *In autumn, the signs of the zodiac take their names and qualities from the zodiacal constellations which the Sun occupies.*

I remain unconvinced of this author's premise, since, as we shall see, there are elements in the Prussian zodiacal system which do appear to refer to the sign occupied by the sun and others which clearly refer to the opposite sign, but the system as proposed doesn't work consistently, and the symbolism referring to the sign occupied by the sun or the sign opposite the sun seems to occur at random rather than obeying a set pattern

December 21–January 21
The Golden Bird (Capricorn)

The beginning of the year took place upon the night of the winter solstice. This was the night upon which Peckols, the Prussian Velnias who ruled the world of the dead, led his armies of ancestral spirits into battle against the forces of darkness to restore the power of the waning sun. The Prussian name for this zodiacal sign was *Aūss Pippelis* (the Golden Bird). Small straw birds were hung in people's houses during the winter solstice holidays. The Prussians believed that the creator aspect of Dievs or Dievas, called *Autrīmpus*, took the form of a loon and dove into the primeval ocean to gather up earth for the creation of the world. This was the bird of straw that hung in common houses and, in the mythic sense, a truly "golden" bird, signifying the creation of the world and therefore referring to the sign which the sun occupies rather than its opposite; it gives us the message that the beginning of the year was symbolic of the beginning of the world, that the world itself is reborn each year. The quality associated with this sign is *gīwan* (life), which could be said to symbolize the opposite sign, the summer solstice, when life flourishes at its finest, though it could also be taken to refer to the return of the solar life force after it has reached its weakest point.

January 21–February 21
The Wolf (Aquarius)

The Prussian name of the second zodiacal month was *Wīlks* (the Wolf) because this was the time that the wolves prepared for mating. Prussians believed that wolves were the first creatures to organize communities (the pack), and therefore they were our teachers in the art of building community. At carnival inns, groups of patrons greeted visitors with ritualistic but meaningless (i.e., harmless) threats, and the visitors gave gifts of food and drink to the patrons to symbolize their acceptance into the pack, the community. This was also the time that was sacred to the Fire Goddess Gabija; neighbors shared fire with each other to establish good relationships, symbolic of human relationships with the world of the gods. The quality associated with this sign was *pannu* (fire), which seems to refer to the fire ceremony of Gabija, and therefore, the sign is described by the position of the sun rather than its opposite.

February 21–March 21
The Crane (Pisces)

The Old Prussian name for this month was *Gērwi*, which means "Crane," for migratory cranes began to appear in the Baltic lands at this time. Their voices inform the spirits of the dead—who, after their battle to bring back the sun, are still among us—that it will soon be time for them to return to their own world, for the earth will soon reach its time of warmth and greening. Information for the quality associated with this month has unfortunately been lost over time. But since the Milky Way, known as a "road of souls," is also known as The Path of the Cranes, so the association with the return of the ancestral spirits to their own home may well be a core meaning of this sign.

March 21–April 21
Two Suns (Aries)

The beginning of Aries marks the spring equinox and the time of Easter. The Prussian name for this month was *Dwāi Saūlis* (Two Suns) and was associated with a ram's skin. This was the time when Žemyna, the Earth Goddess, was reborn as a young girl. People donned animal masks and led the spirits of their ancestors back to rivers, such as the Daugava, which would carry them to the Underworld. Once again, the quality associated with this sign is missing.

April 21–May 21
Two Deer (Taurus)

This astrological month was symbolized by a man on horseback and was called *Dwāi Ragīngel* (Two Deer). Images on the Grodno cup make the young rider look every bit the warrior, but he carries no weapons, for he is a bridegroom, the aspect of Dievas called *Pergrūbris* in Prussian and *Praamžis* in Lithuanian. He is riding to his wedding with the youthful and beautiful Earth Goddess, Žemyna, at the Festival of Pergrūbri which took place on April 21 or 22 when the world was becoming green again. Heaven and Earth have married, and the pregnant Earth Mother will give birth with Saulė's heavenly fire to help her. The birch trees are budding, and the time of plowing can now begin. The quality associated with this sign was *gal* (death). This appears to be associated with the opposite sign, the time when the spirits of the dead begin to emerge into this world.

May 21–June 21
The Warriors (Gemini)

The month we know as Gemini was known to the Old Prussians as *Ūlintajs* (The Warriors), and like our own sign, Gemini, it was symbolized by the Divine Twins. They were called the *Aświnai* or "horsemen," which is nearly the same as the Vedic term Aśvins. In Old Prussian, their names are *Āušauts* and *Swāikstiks*. Āušauts will marry the Dawn Goddess Āustrini (Saulė's daughter whom we have met under her Lithuanian name of *Aušrinė*) at the end of the month.

This is the last month of spring, associated with *sēimī,* meaning "family," and signifying the quality of fullness and happiness.

June 21–July 21
The Goat (Cancer)

This zodiacal sign is called *Azē* in Prussian, which means "the goat," and is named for the sign opposite the one which is occupied by the sun, which of course is Capricorn, the goat. This is the time when Saulė has reached her fullness and is turned back upon her course by Ragana the Witch Goddess. The goat is a symbol of cosmic law because goats draw the chariot of Perkūnas, known in Prussian as *Perkūns.* June 24 is his sacred day. It is associated with the quality of *swāikstan* (light), which could refer either to the longest days and the most abundant light, as with the sign which the sun occupies, or to the return of the light at the winter solstice in the opposite sign of the Golden Bird.

July 21–August 21
The Horse (Leo)

The Old Prussian name for this zodiacal constellation is *Zirgs,* which means "the horse." Once again, we are in the presence of the Divine Twins, though this time, we meet them transformed into horses to draw the chariot of Saulė, the Sun Goddess. Like the Western astrological sign Leo, Zirgs is dedicated to the sun. It is associated with the quality of *lads* (ice), which symbolizes the wintry cold of the opposite sign, the Wolf.

August 21–September 21
The Crane (?) (Virgo)

Unfortunately, there is a gap in our knowledge here, and we don't know the Old Prussian name for this sign. Some modern Neopagans in Poland call it *Gērwi,* "the crane," like its opposite sign because in this month, the cranes are preparing to migrate south for the winter, and their departure will mark the beginning of the season when the dead return and walk among us. As we have seen when we considered Pisces, the Milky Way, known as a "road of souls," is also known as "The Path of the Cranes," so the association with the appearance of the ancestral spirits may once again be a core meaning of this sign.

September 21–October 21
The Ram (Libra)

When the sun enters this sign, the autumn equinox takes place. The sign for this zodiacal month is called *Awwins* (ram), a reference to the antipodal or opposite sign. In archaeological materials, its representation is the balance of two suns—two powerful goddesses, Saulė and Māra. The latter is perceived here as an aspect of the Earth Goddess, Žemyna. From the solstice, Māra receives energy from Saulė and bestows it upon the plants. At this time the Earth Goddess, whether we perceive her as Māra or Žemyna, must begin her own journey to the Underworld, for winter is coming and the time of growth is over. The quality associated with this sign is *undan* (water), which seems to describe the opposite month and its springtime rains.

October 21–November 21
Pergrūbris (Scorpio)

In the eleventh month, the sun enters the sign known to Old Prussians as *Pergrūbris*. In Prussian iconography, this sign is depicted as two deer, a reference which appears to be to the opposite sign of the zodiac, which is named "Two Deer" and which is the month during which the festival of Pergrūbris takes place. At the beginning of the month (in what we would call early November, corresponding to the Days of the Dead), the Prussian Welinnis Festival (Lithuanian *Velinas*) initiated the season when the spirits of the dead return to the earth. During this festival, Old Prussians believed that Māra became the bride of Peckols (Velnias) and therefore the Queen of the Underworld. The quality associated with this sign is *zemē* (earth), perhaps a reference to Māra as the Earth Goddess and her sojourn in the Underworld, or perhaps a reference to the opposite sign when the Earth Mother is married.

November 21–December 21
The Horsemen (Sagittarius)

The twelfth and last sign of the zodiac was known in Old Prussian as *Ašwinai.* Once again, we are with the Divine Twins as horsemen. This sign's symbol is the warrior, depicted as an armed man on horseback, thus bearing some resemblance to the Western Sagittarius. It probably represents Peckols, the ruler of the Underworld, who must lead the armies of the dead into battle against the forces of chaos to rescue Saulė, so that she may return to earth on the night of the solstice. The quality associated with this month is *deiwūtisku* (blessings and good fortune).

Nine

The Winter Festivals

THE WINTER SOLSTICE (DECEMBER 21)

As we have seen, this is the night when Velnias and the armies of the dead go to battle for the sake of Saulė, the Goddess of the Sun. She has reached the lowest point of her light. The nights are long and cold. This is the night of the rebirth of the sun, the rebirth of light. The rites of the winter solstice predate Christianity by millennia. Though early Church fathers declared that Jesus of Nazareth was born in March or April, the Church later assigned to him a birthdate near the winter solstice, partly to compete with the cult of Mithras, who was also said to have been born at the time of the winter solstice, and partly to tie in the Christian mythos with the universal theme of the birth of the light at the darkest time of year. Over the centuries, Pagan winter solstice rites became mixed with the customs of the Christmas season, and at the present time, the solstice and Christmas are a blend of both Paganism and Christianity.

Throughout the dark winter nights of the solstice season, Baltic families spent their evenings next to the household fire. Sons and daughters practiced needlework, and fairy tales were told to the younger children. Riddles were told; answers were guessed.

Christmas Eve was called *Kūčios* in Lithuania, while December 24 through December 26 was known as *Ziemassvetki* in Latvia. At that time, families began to gather together ever more closely. Sometimes the preparations began a full week in advance and involved the entire village. It was the custom for everyone to make peace with their neighbors and to forgive those who had become enemies. Many people avoided the word "I" and said "we," to indicate that everyone in the village was included. Fasting was common, as was bathing in the "household shrine" of the sauna. A person must sit at the Christmas table clean in every sense, without bad thoughts. A true Lithuanian Christmas not only has almost nothing to do with Christian tradition, it is a celebration of community solidarity in all its aspects. The celebration of this solidarity includes not only the family in the broadest sense but also the community of the living and the dead and the household serpent integrated into the family. Christmas food is shared not only with domestic animals and bees but also with fruit trees.

On Christmas Eve, the entire house had to be thoroughly cleaned; all the bed linens had to be changed. Everyone attending the Christmas Eve dinner had to bathe and dress in clean clothes. Everyone who was absent from their village of origin made a concerted effort to be home for Christmas Eve, no matter how far they had traveled. The rites practiced at that time were intended to draw the entire family—and indeed, the entire community—together in a sacred spirit. If a family member had died during the year or had reasons serious enough to prevent them from returning home, an empty space was left at the table for them. A plate and a chair marked the person's seat, though the utensils were not put out. A small candle was placed on the plate and lit during the meal. Thus, even those absent or deceased could participate in the all-important meal.

The winter solstice was a time of wealth and abundance. The granary was full with the fruits of the autumn harvest. Nevertheless, it was common for people to fast and abstain from meat on December 24. This was a Pagan custom, observed as a spiritual practice. The Catholic church tried to put an end to ritual fasting, but without much success. Even now, most Lithuanians refrain from meat on Christmas Eve.

The table was prepared in a special way. It was covered with a pure white linen tablecloth. This custom also marked the autumnal observances for the return of the spirits of the family ancestors, of which we shall hear more later on. Plates were decorated with sigils symbolizing the life force that sustains the harmony of the world. The table was smudged with juniper and sprinkled with water that had been preserved since Easter. Boughs of fir and candles were also laid out as symbols of the life force, though fresh flowers were never used, especially the red or white poinsettias so common in ceremonies at other times of the year.

An effort was made to have as much light as possible in the house—not only for the Christmas Eve dinner but throughout the solstice holidays. Lanterns and candles abounded. A birch log was the local "Yule Log" of the Baltic and was kept burning in the fireplace at all times. No fire was allowed to go out.

Dinner began when the first star appeared in the sky, though the night was often so cloudy as to hide all stars, in which case the head of the household simply announced the beginning of the meal.

In Pagan times, the earth goddesses and gods and the Underworld spirits were invoked by the head of the household, who knelt upon the earth, filled three cups with beer, and passed them around to all the members of the household. Then he placed a loaf of bread upon the ground and spoke the evening prayer:

"Father Earth, you give us good bread and we thank you for it. Help us with your blessings when we work the earth, so that with your help and the help of Mother Earth we may receive more of your blessings."

Then he raised the loaf of bread above him and said: "Fill us up."

Then he poured more of the ceremonial beer upon the ground, drank from the cup, and said:

"Mother Earth, beautiful flower, raise up the work we do with our hands."

Then a final cup of beer was passed around. Everyone drank from it.

Among the many foods that were consumed at the solstice or Christmas Eve meal, no meat was eaten. In many regions throughout the Baltic, dairy and hot foods were also avoided.

In Latvia, peas and beans were common because it was said that they brought prosperity. Though meat was generally forbidden, fish was not, and herring was frequently served with sauces based in tomato, mushroom, or onion. Eel was another common fish dish. Baked potatoes, sauerkraut, biscuits, and cranberry bread were among the dishes. A multi-grain bread was eaten with honey because butter was a dairy product and therefore not allowed. Borscht, cabbage, apples, nuts, and cookies with poppyseed milk were popular as well.

After the dinner, the mother of the family sprinkled grain upon the family members, especially the children. The father sprinkled it upon the fireplace. It was said that the spirits of the ancestors bestowed a special magic upon the grain so that it gave supernatural assistance to the entire family.

The household's animals were kindly treated as well. Hay which had formed part of the dinner table decoration, honoring the ancestors, was later fed to the animals. A mixture of wheat and peas was sprinkled in the barn to ensure their good health for the following year. When the house was washed in preparation for the ceremonial meal, the wash water was given to the animals and was believed to protect them from the evil eye. The Lithuanians called upon the *žaltys* snakes who lived beneath the stove or in the sauna as household guardians to come forth and taste of the food.

When all was finished, the family went to bed but left food and beer on the table all night long so that the spirits of their ancestors could feast in their own fashion.

Yuletide or the winter solstice season was marked by vigorous festivity in former days. On the eve of the new moon nearest to the solstice, young people gathered for a "New Moon Festival" in which the girls brewed a concoction of crushed poppies, hemp, honey, and liqueur. They invited the young men to drink their fill of it, and it was a party that typically lasted most of the night. In Latvia, fir trees were decorated with ribbons, dried flowers, dollies woven of straw, and fruits. One rather jolly *daina* proclaims:

Waiting for the Yuletide,
I brewed a sweet beer.
Wonderful Yuletide,
Three blessed days.[42]

Priests and other dedicated Christians raged against such celebrations, which they claimed were characterized by "shameless" feasting, eating, drinking, dancing, jumping, and shouting. They howled that the Latvians spent the entire night dancing and leaping about. During medieval and Renaissance times, and even later, young men from the professional guild houses in Riga erected a large fir tree in the Market Square and decked it out with roses. Crowds of women, described by the churchmen as "both wives and virgins," indulged themselves with songs and games while the young merchants danced a ring dance around the tree. But though pastors and priests howled at such Pagan ways, no one paid any attention to their Christian outrage.

Perhaps the most lively, vivid, and thoroughly Pagan of all the winter solstice festivities were the masked processions. Such processions still survive in parts of Europe today. From place to place, there were many associations with many names that conducted such processions. The masquers dressed as gypsies, beggars, bears, cranes, horses, and of course, Death. Some masquers even changed their voices so that they wouldn't be recognized by their neighbors. They marched from one village to the next, and it was considered a blessing if such a procession visited your home, for they were said to drive away evil spirits. They were likely to inspect your house to ensure that everything was in order, that the master and the mistress, sons and daughters, and even the children were all fulfilling their conventional duties. They made certain the house was clean and tidy.

Sometimes, the leader of a masked procession carried a staff which was regarded as magical. To touch it was to receive the power of life which was reborn with Saulė's turning northward on the solstice. Those who were deemed by other family members to be lazy or contentious might very well get a spanking with the masque master's rod. Such a pummeling was believed to promote fertility and health and to protect the victim from sickness and bad magic.

My daughter-in-law is a lazy slut,
Come on, lads, and spank her!
She can't be bothered to spin the flax,
Spank her, lads, as hard as you can![43]

To point out that the masked processions are thoroughly Pagan in origin is a virtual redundancy. Shani Oates, the Maid of the Traditional Witchcraft associated Clan of Tubal Cain, remarks:

> *"Masks are the oldest expression of humanity. They retain the element of mystery, inculcating uncertainty within the onlooker... They adopt a public face by hiding the private one; they transform, protect, scare, intimidate, shock, all by inversion! Masks generate transformation in the viewers' mind; for the wearer of such a tool, this is immensely empowering. It is also liberating... We know them not and therefore cannot hold them to account; essentially they are beyond the bounds of Law. Do we ask or answer the puzzles and mysteries suggested by their antics and posturing? Do we imagine they are pointing the finger at us? Can they read our minds?.... [It] calls to attention the often overlooked yet vital reasons why animal guising and masking was considered such an abomination by the Church... So sacrilegious, in fact, it was rendered the worst offence [sic] simply because it mocked nature, God's perfect creation, it violated the divine, in both Pagan and Christian celebrations during 'mundus inversus' (the earth inverted) that is, when it is ruled by the Devil!"* [44]

Divination was characteristic of all the Baltic holidays, but especially the winter solstice. At this turning of the year, time and space were free of their ordinary limitations, and the world, renewed by the battle prowess of the Underworld Lord, was once again in its primordial state. The ancestor spirits were at large in the world of the living, and the ancestors know of hidden things.

Perhaps the most common types of divination were performed by young women to ascertain whom they would marry.

> *A clump of hay is pulled from under the tablecloth. It cannot be chosen; the first strand that the girl's fingers encounter must be drawn. If a long, slender stalk is withdrawn, the girl can expect a tall slender husband, while a short, fat, bent stalk means a short, fat, crooked husband.*

> *Every girl in the room must light a candle. All the candles will be placed on the table's edge and blown out by the master of the house. If a girl's candle is not blown out, she will remain unmarried.*

A ring is dropped into a half-filled glass of water by a young woman. Count the number of ripples it produces, for that will show the number of years before she is married.

Let a girl eat three herrings without any breading just before she goes to bed. Place two wooden rods in her bedroom, and a towel over the rods. Place a bowl of water under the rods and the towel, and the whole thing next to her bed. She will dream of her future husband.

Take six small bags and place an item in each one—a coin, a piece of coal, a lump of earth, a ring, grain or seeds, and a small rag. Place the bags in a tub next to the girl's bed, close enough so that she can reach it without getting out of bed. When she wakes up, let her grab a bag. The ring means she will be married, money means she will be wealthy, coal warns of a fire in the house, earth means she will die young, the rag represents children, while the seeds or grains represent a good harvest.

And, inevitably in a farming community, there were many predictions regarding next year's weather and crops.

When the trees are covered with snow after Christmas, the plants that bloom around the summer solstice will do well.

If it's cold around the winter holidays, it will be hot in the summer.

If there is a lot of snow around the winter holidays, it will rain around Midsummer.

If the snow is deep on Christmas Day, wet weather can be expected at Midsummer, but if the snow is shallow, the haying weather at Midsummer will be glorious.

If there is beautiful weather around Christmas, then there will also be beautiful weather around Midsummer.

If it freezes at Christmas, then next summer there will be good haying weather.

The Tschagattas

Masked and costumed festivals are still held in various parts of Europe, typically in February. I have encountered them in Maastricht, Holland, and Basel, Switzerland. While all of them are for the most part secularized now, it is clear that they originated in Pagan rituals that marked the return of the ancestral spirits—who have been here in the world of the living since the end of autumn—to their own Underworld realm. The most thoroughly Pagan example I have seen is the ceremony of the Tschagatta (an Alpine dialectical word for "witches") in the village of Blatten in the Lotschental Valley of Switzerland. The village men who portray the *tschagatta* spend the entire year creating their elaborate costumes made of goatskins and hung with silver bells, all of them distinguished by a fearsome, demonic-looking mask which they themselves have fashioned. Local legend says that even into Renaissance times, there was a Pagan village on one side of the Lotschental and a Christian village on the other. The Pagans lived on the shady side of the valley and often raided the Christian village. The Pagan raiders wore horrific masks which represented the fierce warrior spirits of their ancestors. These were the origin of the *tschagatta* masks. On a day in late February, the citizens of Blatten gather in the village square. The teenage girls of the village—and sometimes their mothers as well! —get wildly drunk on a sickly-sweet blend of wine called *gluwein*. After dark, the men from the Tschagatta Society, clad in their costumes and ferocious masks, begin crossing the valley, from the Pagan side to Blatten, which lies on the Christian side. They appear one by one, seemingly out of nowhere. Suddenly, they are simply there, right in front of you or behind you, rattling their bells and roaring at you. (Of course, they are local villagers and know all the good hiding places.) They grab people at random—sometimes including male tourists but more often than not, women—and drag their inebriated teenage captives (or their equally inebriated mothers) across the village square while the ladies shriek with terror and laughter at the same time. Afterward, the *tschagatta* march to the next village, dance in the central square, then on to the next village, and so on. They appear several times over the next few days, then disappear until February of the next year.

Magical Working

During the week before the Winter Solstice, clean the house until it is spotless. Visit friends and neighbors, paying special attention to making peace and creating harmony with those whom you have quarreled or had unfortunate dealings with during the preceding year.

For Yuletide dinner, decorate the table with a clean white linen cloth. Make sure there is as much light as possible. If you have a fireplace, burn a Yule Log. Set a place at the table for those dear to you who have recently passed, for favorite ancestors, and for dear ones who are unable to join you.

When the first star appears in the sky, let the senior male lead your company out in front of the house and say a prayer to Father and Mother Earth. This can be done indoors if you live in an apartment in the city.

Try to get by with a vegetarian dinner, although fish is acceptable.

In modern times, we are likely to have pets rather than livestock. We now know that "people food" isn't always good for them but do give your pets an appropriate "special treat."

After dinner, let the seers among you break out their tarot cards or runes and enjoy a session of divination for one and all. Questions regarding love and romance are especially favored.

When all is done and it is time for sleep, leave the table settings for the departed as they are, and leave some food for them as well.

METEŅI (FEBRUARY 5–6)

The term *Meteņi* literally means “a throw-away,” and this is when we cast away the things of winter. Though the snow is still deep upon the ground and the weather is still cold, the first hints of spring are beginning to appear and to be celebrated in their own fashion.

Meteņi takes place in the month of the Wolf in the Old Prussian zodiac, and there are some curious songs and sayings that have to do with the idea of young women conquering the wolves, who are cranky at this time of year because of the mating season.

The wolf is howling
In the dark forest grove,
And the maidens are afraid.
But it is not the wolf they fear,
It's the darkness of the night.[45]

It is said that a young woman will wield a whip and drive away the wolves so that they do not attack the farmers' sheep.

As the wolves await the spring, so do us mortals. And though the snowbells now poke their heads up into the light, the ground is thick with snow, and it is time for sledding. To many of us, this may seem like a game rather than a ritual, but our ancestors believed that spiritual observance could be filled with fun and joy.

Sledding parties were an observance intended to promote abundance in next year's harvest, especially flax. The higher the mountain and the faster the ride down, the higher and thicker the flax would grow. The growth of the flax was compared to the excellence of one's father so that young folk sledding down the hills cried out: “Taller than my father! Taller than my father!”

This prelude to the coming spring was echoed in the symbolism of Meteņi folk songs as well.

Horses appear often in such songs, with lines such as: "The horse ran and the grass grew." Here, the galloping horse symbolizes the life force of nature awakening.

Water is also a common symbol in Meteņi songs, for water is the primordial substance from which all things are born, including the abundance of Nature, which moves and flows like a rushing stream.

The ancient Goddess of the Neolithic puts in an appearance in Meteņi songs as well as a maiden sitting in a golden chair on an island in the middle of a rushing stream, combing her hair. Her hair is a symbol of both the flow of life and the growth of the flax.

After the Christianization of the Baltic, the time of Meteņi was also the time just before the strongly enforced custom of fasting for Lent. In some ways, then, Meteņi could be said to resemble our own Mardi Gras, a "carne vale" or "farewell to the flesh" preceding a time of asceticism. In the Baltic, therefore, Meteņi became a time of lavish feasts in which everyone deliberately over-ate. Beer, meat, and pies were consumed in abundance, and pork was particularly important. A mixture of groats, beans, peas, and pork was one of the specialties of the festival time.

Though men and women feasted, they did not feast alone, for the spirits of the ancestors were still abroad upon the earth and the pure linen tablecloths that honored them were still in use. By the time of the spring equinox, they would depart, but in Meteņi, they were still present in our human world.

The masked processions which had begun in the autumn festivals of Mikeli or Mārtiņi were held one last time in Meteņi before they ended for the rest of the year. Once again, the costumed villagers in their usual garb—the gypsy, crane, beggar, bear, and goat—would visit all the village houses to bless the people with fertility, abundance, and prosperity. Once again, the masked visitors danced, although on Meteņi the mistress of the house danced with them, and her dancing was considered especially auspicious. In some parts of Lithuania, two members of the masked fraternities would dress up as Lašininis and Kanapinis (winter and spring) and hold a mock battle, which Kanapinis was sure to win.

And, as usual, there was divination, with plenty of weather forecasting that concerned the coming Easter (the vernal equinox).

What is the weather like in Meteņi, it will be like that on Easter as well.

If there is snow on the roof in Meteņi, it will also be there on Easter.

If it rains on Meteņi and the rooster can drink from it, then it will be a good year.

If the moon is three days old on the day of Meteņi, it will be a good year. If it is older, it will be a bad year.

Magical Working

If you live in a region where there is a great deal of snow, hold a sledding contest.

Celebrate with a feast. If you are not a vegetarian, include pork.

As at the winter solstice, use a spotless white linen tablecloth to honor the ancestors and set a place for them at the table.

Bring out your divination tools after dinner.

Perhaps the most deeply religious aspect of Meteņi was the ceremony held in honor of Gabija the Fire Goddess. As mentioned in Chapter Three, a candle was carried three times around the kitchen table or the fireplace of each home. Also, the sigil of Perkūnas was marked upon the forehead, back of the head, and behind the ears of all family members—especially the children—to keep them safe from the Thunder God's bolts of lightning. It also protected the children from disease and disaster.

Magical Working

If you have not exchanged fire with like-minded friends by bringing a candle with you on a visit to their homes and lighting it to give them the gift of fire, you may do so now.

Ten

The Springtime Festivals

THE VERNAL EQUINOX
EASTER (MARCH 21)

In the present day, Christians associate Easter with the resurrection of Christ, but ritual and ceremony at this time of year long predate Christianity. In ancient times, the vernal equinox—which English speakers call "Easter" in honor of Eostre, the Anglo-Saxon goddess of spring and the equinox—was celebrated as the resurrection of the year itself, and therefore of life itself. On the vernal equinox, day and night are equal. The light and the darkness are balanced, but it is the light which will increase and grow stronger. Easter is then celebrated to honor the arrival of spring and the sun, the triumph of light over darkness, and its rituals help awaken the earth.

Historical sources show that until the Middle Ages, Easter was celebrated for an entire week, but was later limited to three days. In contemporary times, the celebrations are a mixture of Christian and Pagan Baltic traditions, though the Pagan element remains the strongest. This was the time when Žemyna, the Earth Goddess, was reborn as a young girl. By the time the day and night are equal, the earth is green enough for Žemyna, who has been sleeping below the ground while the world is frozen and cold, to be born again—resurrected—as a beautiful young woman, still untouched and virginal. In the Pagan metaphor, which envisioned human life as the progression of the seasons, the vernal equinox is our birth and our childhood, just as it is the Earth Mother's. The vernal equinox is also the time when the souls of the dead, who have been with us here on earth since the autumn festivals, must return to their own world as a new cycle begins in the world of the living.

On Easter morning, one must rise early to greet the sun and bathe in the water of a running stream that flows towards the sun—which is to say, an eastward flowing stream. The simple act of bathing in a stream is a magical ritual of purification that helps us grow vitality, clarity of mind, health, and beauty.

But the night and the time of darkness are still strong even as the light is gaining in power. In contrast to Christmas, when granaries were full and food was abundant, Easter was the time when the granary was nearly empty. The Easter meal was a much more modest affair than that of Christmas, for the winter food supply was running out. What food there was consisted largely of cereal products and milk. There were special dishes, baked in rounded forms to represent the sun, such as boiled eggs and peas. Such foods, round like coins, were said to bring wealth. The equinox was also a time when dark magic was still afoot, and the acts of evil spirits and sorcerers were feared.

Among the practices which symbolized the balance of light and dark and the awakening of the world, the decoration of eggs and swinging were the most common and the most popular.

Swinging may seem like an odd sort of Pagan celebration, but it has its symbolism—when we swing back and forth, we imitate the sun traveling from one solstice point to the other, with the equinox represented by the midpoint of our arc. Those who practiced this custom sought out a good place to put the swing: the tops of local hills were favored so that other villagers could see your swing and take note of your activity from a distance. After all, physical forms of expression such as dancing in a circle and leaping over the fire were a part of Pagan ceremony, so why not swinging? Some people built swings and participated in marking the solar progress. Those who built the swings usually did so every year, and it was considered inauspicious if they stopped. At the end of the equinoctial celebrations, the swings were taken down and then burned so that their magical qualities could not be used by sorcerers and evil spirits. Adults and children both participated.

The Metaphysics of Swinging

The symbolic representation of the sun's passage from south (winter solstice) to north (summer solstice) and back again was universal. Among the Maya, the K'iche' word for the solar year is *ab'*, which also means "hammock." When I asked about it, I was told that in a hammock, we swing from one side (one of the solstices) to the other side (the opposite solstice), and when we are mid-swing, we represent the equinoxes. The Maya may not have anything resembling our park swings, but they have hammocks which serve the purpose.

In Hawaii, there is a place called Cape Kumukahi on the Big Island, which is the easternmost point in the island chain, and therefore, the first place at which one may experience the sunrise. At one time, there were two large rocks (which no one now seems able to identify with confidence) which were perceived as two sisters. From the right vantage point, the sun would appear to rise over one or the other stone at the solstices, and it was said that the sisters rolled the sun back and forth from year to year. In the esoteric teachings of hula, the simple hand gesture of moving the arms first to one side and then the other is said to represent the same thing. In hula esotericism, one focuses one's attention on one's *piko,* the source of power and energy behind the navel, also acknowledged universally as a center of spiritual power. (See Chapter One for a description of the inner centers.) Therefore, the dancer is always in the center of all things, representing the equinoxes.

The most famous of all Easter rituals was, of course, the painting of eggs with patterns and symbols that had mystical meanings. In Eastern Europe, such eggs are genuine works of art, rich with cosmological symbolism. The custom, widely practiced in Slavic countries, does not seem to have reached the Amber Coast at a very early date, for there is only one old-fashioned Latvian *daina* about it:

Come now, my sisters,
Let's make speckled eggs.
Let's make ham to eat
When comes the Easter morning.[46]

There were a fair number of traditions regarding eggs. Young lads and lasses exchanged eggs—the fertility element and unspoken eroticism here are hard to miss. Sometimes the girls threw eggs at the boys while they were swinging—even traveling the sacred road of Saulė couldn't stop teenagers from acting like teenagers. Eggs were offered to the gods as a form of protection against negative witchcraft and sorcery. In Latvia, it was said that eating eggs made you grow as round as an egg! (Plump was preferred to thin in medieval times.)

There was yet another use for eggs, and it involved one of the other major cyclic changes in the year.

It is generally agreed, throughout Europe, that the spirits of the ancestors emerge from the Otherworld to live in our mortal world at some point in the autumn—the Celtic Samhain, the origin of our Halloween, is the best-known example. On the Baltic coast, the belief was the same—we shall hear more about it when we study the autumn festivals. There are also variant traditions as to when the dead return to their own world—the ceremonies of Fasnacht and the Tschagatta which I attended in Switzerland took place in late February. In the Baltic, the spring equinox was the time when the ancestors returned home. According to the Old Prussian zodiac, the process began in what we, today, would describe as Pisces (February 21–March 21), which the Old Prussians knew as Gērwi, the sign of the Crane. At this time of year, migrating cranes began to make their appearance along the Amber Coast, and it was said that their cries served as a signal to the ancestors that their time to return to the Otherworld had come.

The sign of Dwāi Saūlis (Two Suns) began on the equinox and was equivalent to our Aries. Then (at least in Prussia, though local customs may have varied), the masked societies donned their costumes once again and led their ancestors on a procession to a sacred river (the Daugava or Dvina in Latvia, which, as we have seen, was the earthly counterpart of the Milky Way, a universal "Road of Souls"). There, the ancestors would enter a spirit boat—perhaps, as in some legends, the boat of Saulė herself—and return to their supernatural home. But they were not forgotten. On Easter, eggs were taken to the graves of one's departed ancestors and left there, so that the spirits of one's beloved predecessors might quickly enter into reincarnation.

If you want to experiment with decorating eggs and are not sure what sort of symbols to use, there are several Baltic sigils which will serve nicely, especially those of Dievas, Laima, Māra, and the rosette of Saulė.

Another fine equinox custom is to take an egg or two to the grave of a favorite deceased relative or friend—one to whom you wish a quick and joyful reincarnation—and leave it there. You can conceal the eggs in a more conventional bouquet of flowers, so that this time people won't think you're crazy.

Magical Working

If you live in a major city instead of the countryside and cannot build your own swing set, you can still go to a local park on the vernal equinox and have a nice time on the swings. If you are an adult, some people may indeed think that you are crazy, but that's their problem.

ÚSIṆI (MAY 5–6)

Nowhere is the syncretic mix between Paganism and Christianity seen more clearly than in the holiday of Úsiṇi. Originally, it was celebrated on May 5 or 6, midway between the vernal equinox and summer solstice, in keeping with the forty-five-day "Times" of the ancient calendar. It was dedicated to the god Úsiṇš, the god of horses, and, like the Celtic Beltane to which it corresponds, it marked the beginning of summer. After the advent of Christianity, however, the holiday began to be celebrated on St. George's Day, April 23, and it received the name *Jurģi*, the Baltic name corresponding to "George." English speakers will recall St. George as the slayer of a dragon—a tale which had absolutely nothing to do with the early Christian who was martyred during the reign of the Roman Emperor Diocletian, but instead, is yet another variant of the universal myth of the heroic god who slays the primal dragon. In European folklore, St. George was a patron saint of horses, as was Úsiņš, and this probably had a great deal to do with the shift of this holiday from the "cross-quarter" time of early May to the feast day of St. George on April 23.

One of the more interesting bits of synchronicity involved with the shift of this early summer festival from May to April 23 lies in the fact that there was another ceremony, called the *Pergrūbri Festival* in Old Prussian, which celebrated one of the most potent and powerful events of the mythic year. As we have seen, the Earth Goddess Žemyna awakened from her winter sleep and reappeared to the woman as a young girl during the time of Easter. Grown to early womanhood now, blossoming like the first buds of the birch trees that appear now, it is time for her to be married to an aspect of Dievas called *Praamžis* in Lithuanian and *Pergrūbris* in Old Prussian. Father Sky and Mother Earth are joined in a rite of sacred marriage which marks the beginning of summer, the time of abundance of the Earth Mother. By yet another bit of synchronicity, the day of their marriage is the day that contemporary ecologists have chosen to celebrate Earth Day.

An Old Prussian description of the Pergrūbri Festival[47] relates that in every village, the people gathered in someone's house. Just before sundown, a plow was brought into the barn where the oxen were kept—they beheld it for the first time that year. Only men attended this part of the ceremony, and they praised the gods and filled their cups three times in honor of Žemyna.

At sundown, a few kegs of beer were put out, and the Pagan priest raised a goblet and prayed to Pergrūbris: "O mighty god, you drive away the winter and make the grass to grow and leaves to come forth in all our lands, and we beseech you now to command our crops to grow, to destroy all the weeds!"

The priest prayed to Perkūnas for rain and to other deities for light, the health of the cattle, the flourishing of fields and pastures. A dish called *warška*, comprised of fatty cottage cheese, cream, butter, egg yolks, coconut flakes, raisins, and honey was served. Then the all-night dancing and partying could begin.

Magical Working

On Earth Day, invite like-minded friends to join you for a party. Begin by pouring out some beer and saying a prayer for Father Sky and Mother Earth.

Entertain with foods such as cheese and cream, coconut flakes, raisins, and honey.

Party with vigor.

Before the coming of Christianity, when the festival of Úsiņi was celebrated upon the "true" cross-quarter days of May 5 or 6, it was dedicated to the god Úsiņš (Latvian). Not only was he the patron deity of horses, but he was also a god of light and of the springtime season, and like Perkūnas, though in a gentler way, a guardian of the cosmic order. Linguists disagree on whether his name is derived from a word meaning "light" or one meaning "guardian of the house." He was the patron of cattle and sheep as well as horses, and of herders and shepherds. Villagers often named the best horse in their herd after him, and the cattle were let out to pasture for the first time upon his festival day. He was also the guardian deity of bees, who were of major importance to the ancient people of the Amber Coast. Around the time of his festival, sowing could begin.

Úsiņš was depicted as a vigorous man with a large, sweeping moustache; he was sufficiently important to have his own sigil.

Since summer was now approaching, Úsiņi was also about preserving beauty and health. Since the birch trees were beginning to bud out, their juice could be extracted, and if it snowed on Úsiņi morning, people washed their mouths with a special birch juice mouthwash. If one were to take up a jolly stance and walk about barefoot while whistling, it was said to protect them from fever during the year. The household oven would often be lit on Úsiņi morning, and smoke rising up the chimney was an auspicious thing. Whoever lit up the family oven first would be made happy.

Magical Working

Walk happily on this first day of spring. Go barefoot and whistle a merry tune.

Sometimes there were negative weather indications for the coming agricultural season. Rain on Úsiņi meant rain throughout the summer and not enough sunlight for the forests to produce their customary healing herbs. If Úsiņi fell on a Monday, the summer would be unhappy, but if on a Friday, it could blight every season of the year. The women did not weave on Úsiņi; to do so would be to produce too much thunder.

Loaves of bread cooked upon Úsiņi had to be circular, for this would help the horses and cows grow fat and round. Eggs were rolled across the backs of cows for the same purpose, while black roosters and hens were sacrificed and eaten to ensure the health of horses and cows.

I promised a thing to Jurgis,
I promised it long ago.
A barrel of beer and some oven bread,
A black rooster and turkey too.[48]

One important matter was that property leases typically expired on April 23, St. George's Day, so during Christian times (about the beginning of the nineteenth century) this was the day when people left their old houses to occupy new ones.

In order to do well and be successful in one's new home, tenants did not say farewell to the old one. Instead, they took straw from the old barn and sprinkled it in the new one as protection against black magic. Stones from the old house were placed in the barn of the new one for the same purpose. Tenants swept the new house immediately upon entering to promote harmony with one's neighbors.

The new tenants cooked cabbage for visitors from other households, which was said to help the new residents to live there for a long time. Eggs were cooked as well so that everyone would live together as peacefully as chickens.

Eleven

The Summer Festivals

THE SUMMER SOLSTICE (JUNE 21)

The summer solstice was perhaps the most important festival of all. It was known in Lithuania as *Rasos* and in Latvia as *Līgosvetki*. Though it begins the festival cycle of summer, it was—and still is—commonly known as *Midsummer*. It was the time when the Goddess Saulė had reached the apex of her power, her light. Thus, in an esoteric sense, it corresponded to the peak of the mountain of Heaven, and in the metaphor of the year as the human life cycle, it was the vigor and strength of late youth and early adulthood. After the advent of Christianity, it became known as the Festival of Saint Jonas in Lithuania and as *Jāņi* in Latvia, because the feast day of John the Baptist fell upon June 24. It was also known as "Medicine Day" and "Medicine Night," for reasons we shall explore.

So powerful was this day that it was said that Saulė herself came down to Earth in human form with her beautiful and erotic daughter

Aušrinė and danced with mortals. Saulė wore red flowers and silver shoes and danced at the top of a silver hill. We have already noted that Saulė, like Dievas and Laima, sometimes disguised themselves as country people and walked with the farmers through their fields, dispensing good advice. Saulė and Aušrinė's descent from the heavenly World Tree to join villagers in the Midsummer dancing is yet another instance of one of the Baltic region's most charming beliefs—the goddesses and gods genuinely like human beings and enjoy our company, especially in times of delight and happiness such as this.

Despite the joy associated with the holiday, however, the summer solstice was the poorest time of the year for the average farmer. The stores of food that had been laid in during the previous autumn were nearly exhausted, and it was yet too early to harvest the new crops that had been planted in the spring. Nevertheless, people went to great lengths to create a festive mood. The farms were decked out with branches of oak, rowan, linden, and birch, and with meadow flowers. Alder and aspen were never used for such decorations; they were considered inauspicious for that purpose.[49] The men brewed beer; the women made cheese. The house, the barn, and even the road of approach were all swept clean. Gardens were weeded, trees were trimmed, and firewood was cut for the bonfires that would light up the solstice eve. Sigils were carved upon the doors of house and barn alike.

Sometimes it was feared that those who considered the village an "enemy" might cast spells to blight the crops; therefore, protective charms were common. Thistles, nettles, and thorns were hung in the corners, walls, roof, and doors of the barn so that those who tried to cast spells against one's animals would get themselves tangled in the sharp thorns and nettles.

Plants in general were believed to have great power during the summer solstice, and this was the time of year when the special healing properties of herbs were at their best—thus "Medicine Day" and "Medicine Night." The gathering of special plants began well before the event itself, though there were some that were gathered only on Midsummer's Eve after dark, which were said to have the most potent healing qualities, as well as those gathered on Midsummer morning in the dew—which was regarded as an extremely magical substance. Herbaceous plants such as bedstraw, cow wheat, vetchling, and clover were very much favored. Twigs of rowan were often tied together in bundles and used to fumigate the rooms of children, for rowan was said to have the power to cure sickness, anxiety, or black magic in young ones. After Christianization, when the rites of Midsummer became associated with St. John the Baptist, St. John's Wort was also a favorite healing plant.

Many flowers, grasses, and leaves were woven into wreaths to be worn as crowns. Wreaths fashioned for women were generally comprised of flowers, grasses, and herbs. It was said that wreaths braided with twenty-seven—or sometimes thirty-nine—different kinds of flowers and herbs would keep away disease, disaster, and black magic. Oak leaves were the special province of the young men; as the sacred tree of Perkūnas, the oak was quintessentially masculine and a symbol of physical strength, as well as a bringer of good fortune with horses and bees. Like the round cheese that was also made at this time, and like the sacred bonfire of Midsummer Eve itself, the circular shape of the wreath was a symbol of Saulė the sun.

We have noted the masked processions that took place during other festivals, but during the summer solstice, there were processions of singers rather than masquers. They began as early as two weeks before Midsummer and continued until Māras Day on August 5 or 6, though the height of their activity took place on Midsummer Night's Eve. In Latvian, the singers were called *līgotais*, hence the name *Līgo* for this holiday in Latvia. The singers, with their *līgošana* or "līgo songs," were welcomed at each house, for it was said that their visits brought fertility, harvest blessings, health, and happiness. The songs were special and sung only at that time of year. They were offered cheese and beer in gratitude for their visits.

Magical Working

To prepare for the summer solstice, clean and decorate your house. If you live in a region where you can decorate with oak, rowan, linden, birch, and meadow flowers, so much the better. Though our culture doesn't have special solstice songs, you can make it a time of music nonetheless by encouraging all the musicians and singers among you to practice their talents. Any kind of music which is fun and uplifting is favorable, especially when performed at a party featuring beer and cheese. Make wreaths which function as crowns of flowers for one and all. Women typically used a variety of flowers, while men used a basis of oak twigs decorated with flowers.

Though the sun never set on Midsummer Eve, the mellowing of the afternoon light told everyone that the evening had come and it was time for the main event—the lighting of the bonfires. The custom of lighting bonfires for the summer solstice eve is widespread throughout Europe and surely belongs to the earliest possible stratum of European mythology and Pagan ritual. Each village chose the highest hilltop nearby, for it was considered auspicious for the fires to be visible, not only to the entire village but to other nearby villages as well. The light of the fire brought spiritual power and agricultural fertility to the fields and the people upon which it shone. It transmitted its energy into the coming year. The Midsummer fires took the place of the sun, Saulė herself, so that even though she dipped to the horizon near midnight, there was not a single moment in which light did not shine.

And of course, the villagers leapt over the fire with joyful and vigorous bounds, for this was said to bestow good luck and health on the participants throughout the coming year. The people made every effort not to fall asleep; it was auspicious to keep watch over the light during this longest day and shortest night of the year. Sometimes the men would rush to the nearest stream or lake, take off their clothes, and swim naked through the water while the women watched and cheered.

There was a strong erotic element in the old Midsummer rites, and the Christians roared and ranted against it, though without any success.

Nuts grow together in pairs.
Cloves grow together in pairs.
Young people gather in pairs,
On Midsummer Night they do.[50]

Young people did indeed wander into the woods together, there to explore the erotic possibilities—some with marriage in mind, others simply for the joy of it. There are many erotic *dainas* and *dainos* in the repertoire, some of which relate to Midsummer's Eve and some of which are remarkably graphic and lewd even by modern standards. Here is a much longer *daina* than usual, one which expresses the erotic sentiments in a gentle way:

There were two girls behind the hill,
Both of them innkeeper's daughters.
One had sweet beer and the other sour brandy.
The village boys went drinking every evening.
And the girls say,
"You drink and you pay.
Drink a lot, pay a lot,
Time to go home."
And the girls say,
"Drink a lot, drink too much,
We can be nice and walk you home.
We can walk you up the hill,
To a place just made for us.
A bed of pine, a fir tree roof,
A pillow for our heads.
Sit down and let me taste your mouth.
Because we're young, because we're young,
Nothing's ever wrong with love.
Nothing's ever wrong with lust."[51]

Nor was it simply the young who partook of love's pleasures during this shortest night of the year. Wives wore wreaths just like younger women. And both wives and husbands turned their heads when the spouse disappeared into the forest, perhaps for a liaison with that absolutely fascinating neighbor who had been an object of interest all year.

On Midsummer's Night
I didn't know—
A wife or a daughter,
Both wore garlands green.[52]

Such encounters were not considered "cheating" in the modern, ordinary sense of the term. Instead, there was magic in such love-meets, for the passion produced thereby was said to raise the energy of nature in general, and of the coming harvest in particular.

Magical Working

The summer solstice is a great time to gather your friends together and rent a camping space in the nearest national forest or state park. Be courteous to other campers by finding a space which is not too close to them, for they will wish to sleep but you will not.

Light a nice big bonfire in the fire grill and bring enough firewood to make sure that it burns all night long.

It is traditional to leap over the fire, but it may be best not to attempt this unless you actually know what you are doing. Be careful!

Though you will be staying awake all night long and therefore, you won't really need a tent, tents (or at least some big thick blankets) can be helpful for those who wish to experience the erotic dimension of the summer solstice.

One of the best-known legends associated with the eroticism of the summer solstice was that of the fire-fern, for those who wandered into the woods together often claimed to be in search of this magical plant. It was said to bloom only upon Midsummer Eve and was notoriously difficult to find. But for those who could obtain it, all wishes and dreams would come true. This was "Medicine Night" indeed!

There were ways in which an aspirant might prepare to seek the magical flower of the fire-fern. A common method was to mount a broomstick, then dance in a circle, eight times eight, without speaking or laughing. Silly though the method may seem, laughter was strictly forbidden. If one can complete this ritual, it is time to hop astride the broom toward the nearest fern patch—this was a rite which was sometimes undertaken in partnership and sometimes alone, without a lover—and perhaps, if one were lucky, one might find the magic fire-fern. Those who were somewhat less energetic might choose to lie beneath a clump of ferns, then wait until midnight to see if one of them blossomed into the fire-fern.

No matter how one chooses to approach the quest, one must be constantly on guard and well protected by magic, for the fern was guarded by terrifying demons.

And what awaited those who found the fire-fern? It blooms with silver, gold, and diamond blossoms, and is thus a source of extraordinary wealth. One could also acquire magical abilities as a seer, knowing the secrets of the past and the future. For those who find it, everything they wish will come true.

Put it in your shoes and you will be transported wherever you desire to go, and no one else will ever know. You can control demons, discover buried treasure, and attract any lover. It was said that even kings had to bow to the possessor of the fire-fern. One may bring distant or even invisible people to full recollection merely by wishing it.

In time, the growth of new light would signal the advent of Midsummer's Day, the beginning of a new summer season. The morning dew upon this day was said to contain amazing powers for healing, and thus the people would greet the morning sun, then wash their faces with the dew from the grass. Some would go so far as to garb themselves in white, gather the water of the dew, mix it with honey, then wash one's eyes and feet to protect them from all harm.

And yet deeper, darker forces were at work precisely at the moment that mortals celebrated the sun's rejuvenating glory. Saulė had reached the apex of her power, and she gloried in descending unto earth and dancing in joy with mortal men and women.

And yet it was time now for her power to wane. If Saulė's magic were left to grow unchecked, the world would become too hot. The forests would proliferate until they overwhelmed the fields. The crops would wither in the heat. So it was now, precisely on Saulė's day of glory, that the Witch Goddess Ragana acquired the power to bring her solar abundance to halt. She had reached the northernmost point of her journey, and now Ragana would turn her back, send her down a different road, traveling south to the colder, darker times of the Winter Solstice.

For all things must remain in balance, even the Light.

Magical Working

When the morning comes, gather up the morning dew, mix it with honey, and wash your face and feet.

MĀRAS (AUGUST 5, 6)

There is but little that is written concerning the Day of Māras, and that which has been recorded simply tells us that it was a day for blessing and honoring the things which are typically associated with her—children were blessed, the family farm and its animals were honored, there was (as usual) a great deal of food, and there were rituals aimed at the acquisition of prosperity, for Māra was also a goddess of money and the activities of the marketplace.

And yet the mysteries which surround her origin seem also to have surrounded her festivals. For one thing, there were more than a few days devoted to Māra. They were celebrated on March 25, July 2, August 15, and September 8. All of these days have come from Christian holidays in honor of the Virgin Mary, with whom Māra was so often identified.

Once again, the question arises: Was Māra an ancient Neolithic goddess, perhaps even an aspect of Laima, who became symbolically linked with the Virgin Mary after Christianity made its appearance?

Or was it the other way around? Was Mary simply re-envisioned as an old-fashioned Latvian goddess?

One would hope that folk songs—so revealing in so many ways—could provide us with an answer. But there are few *dainas* that relate to the festival of Māras.

In the cycles of forty-five days, her festival would have fallen upon August 5 or 6. But as with Úsiņi, which rightfully ought to have corresponded with the Celtic Beltane but was moved to St. George's Day on April 23, the principal festival for Māra was held on August 15, which happens to be the Christian holiday of the Assumption of Mary.

We know that an early rye harvest took place at that time and that a special rye bread was baked in village ovens. We know that predictions about the weather were common, as were ceremonies devoted to prosperity and economic well-being, but once more, Māra has hidden herself behind veils of myth, religion, and the blending of the two.

Twelve

The Autumn Festivals

THE AUTUMN EQUINOX: APJUMĪBAS MIKELI (SEPTEMBER 21)

This is the time of the harvest festival, a joyous and celebrative time indeed when the fruits of the year's labors are ready to be brought to the granaries, and from thence to the tables. The god who presided over this joyous event was Jumis, whom we have already met (in Chapter Three) as the Harvest Lord.

Once again, Christianity has muddled the days. The original name of this harvest festival celebrates the god Jumis, though the term *Mikeli* refers to the archangel Michael, whose feast day was held upon September 29, a date which came to mark this festival in Christian times.

In the cycle of human life, the autumnal equinox corresponds to the years of our maturity when we have passed the uncertainties of youth and achieved a mellow wisdom, as well as the time of our greatest strength and material well-being.

Jumis had jurisdiction over all the abundance given to us by the land—including beer, which was brewed prolifically at this time. Because this was the most fruitful time of year, it was the festival which featured the most opulent feasts. Singing was common, with joyful and celebrative tunes to match the spirit of the season. Villagers gave each other gifts of flowers at this time. But before a family could begin its own meal, a bit of each dish had to be offered up to the household gods.

When the time came for the year's harvest to be brought in, a woman was chosen to lead other villagers into the fields to gather the crops. This honor often went to the woman who was either the mistress of the farm or the best reaper. She led other villagers into the fields carrying a large phallus made of an uncut bunch of grain tied into a knot and topped with a stone. The people sang songs as they made their way into the fields to gather the crops.

When the last of the harvest has been reaped, the last remaining handful was called the *Jumi*. This final product of the harvest was examined carefully. If insects were discovered and hurried back to hide amongst the earth, it was a good omen for the future. The same was said of other creatures which might escape from the final handful of Jumi, including mice and frogs, for such critters were regarded as protected by Jumis himself. This final handful was blessed and then stored away in the granary.

Though the Harvest Lord is an ancient Neolithic deity who clearly predates Indo-European times, his name as we know it now derives from the Proto-Indo-European word *yemo*, meaning "twin." Special importance was attached to "twin" plants, two growing from one source, such as two fruits, two flowers, or two ears of corn growing upon the same stalk. To find such a plant during the festival of Jumis was regarded as a harbinger of fertility and well-being for those lucky enough to discover it.

Wreaths were woven, as were belts, and the best ones were believed to be those that contained the twins, the Jumis stalks. Such wreaths could be used for magical activities, for it was said that they contained the spirit of Jumis himself. The wreaths and belts were carried to the homes of those upon whose land the "twins" had been found, and the wreath was placed upon the head of the lady of the household while the belt was tied round the landlord's waist.

But despite the festive mood, the spirit of Jumis was not forgotten. Even after the "last" handful was gathered and inspected, some grain was always left in the fields. If a field is completely empty without a single patch of grain, Jumis will feel neglected and forgotten. He may leave your fields, taking his vibrancy, his laughter, and his abundance with him. If you leave a patch of grain still standing, he will know you have not forgotten him.

The reapers of the harvest were not the only people who sought "twin" plants. Young lovers searched for them eagerly, and young women without a lover hunted for them as well.

The autumn equinox was a particularly auspicious time for women to seek a husband because the quality of abundance which characterized the seasonal festival was believed to bless the men of the village. Those who were regarded as especially fine prospects were called "bread fathers," the kind of spouse that village girls hoped for.

There are three drums perched
On the top of the gate.
Girls, take note.
For this is where bread fathers be.[53]

Young maidens sought the "twin" plants, for it was said that if one was found, the girl would be married. The maidens also took close notice of insects that they encountered while searching in the fields. While we, in our modern society, would seldom describe any type of insect as "beautiful," the Pagans of the Amber Coast saw things differently. Insects were part of the world and shared in the world's beauty; there were some that were regarded as particularly fine. Insects were regarded as an embodiment of fertility, and if a young woman discovered a bug that was believed to be beautiful, she would marry a beautiful man.

The time for marriage was running short. Up until the autumn equinox, young men could offer proposals of marriage to women they loved, but after that day, there were to be no more proposals until the next year. On the autumn equinox, the men drank plenty of beer and chased plenty of girls.

The season was changing. The spirits of the departed ancestors were now beginning to emerge from the Underworld, to remain until the spring equinox came again. The winter would be a time for reflection rather than for the exuberance of marriage.

During Meteņi, which took place during the Old Prussian zodiacal month of the Wolf, songs were sung of young women conquering wolves to defend the village livestock. But in a symbiosis of the world of humans and the world of animals, which many of us moderns may find it difficult to understand, after Apjumības, the wolves were left alone to roam free and take what they could find.

Magical Working

Most of us live in cities now and no longer lead a life devoted to agriculture, but one may still honor the traditions of the autumn equinox in their own way.

Have a party to celebrate the abundance of the season. Make sure that beer is on the menu. Before partaking in any food, set aside a bit of it for the ancestors and the spirits who inhabit the home.

Make sure that music is a part of the gathering. Anyone who has an instrument should bring it, and anyone who has a voice should sing along.

If you've been sitting on the fence about a relationship, now would be a good time to make a decision.

MĀRTIŅI (NOVEMBER 5, 6)

Mārtiņi marks the beginning of winter.

We have now reached the end of the forty-five-day cycle called "Laundry Time," which refers to the spotless white linen which must be placed upon tables to honor the ancestors and provide them with a clean place to eat with the rest of us, for they have been emerging from the Underworld since the autumn equinox and are among us now. The original name of this holiday seems not to be known, since "Mārtiņi" is named for *St. Martin of Tours,* whose feast day is on November 10.

This is the end of the economic year. Business will resume as usual when the weather clears. The masked processions which ended in Meteņi begin during Mārtiņi, with village societies roaming from house to house garbed as bears, cranes, goats, "the tall wife," "the short man," and the spirit of Death. In a certain sense, all of them represent ancestor spirits. Some wear their fur coats inside out and challenge themselves by placing bundles of briars beneath their armpits. As usual, they go from house to house, dance about, and scare the village children.

It is not difficult to know when such a procession is about to arrive, because the Mārtiņi masked dancers bang on pot lids, pans, and drums. Their approach is quite noisy. When they enter a house, they snoop around, checking to make sure that everything is in order, and clean. They are likely to make sure that the children are obedient, and the daughters are diligent in their appointed tasks. For those who are remiss, there are spankings, just as during the winter solstice, and again with the intent of bestowing strength and good health upon those who receive such a paddling.

The masked societies danced on Mārtiņi, kicking their feet vigorously in order to drive away any unpleasant spirits who might be lingering in the household. They spoke in mocking, joking phrases. It was traditional to honor the masquers by serving them a thick porridge with meat, which awaited them in a large pot on the stove.

They were appreciative of a good meal set before them:

Here we were kindly welcomed,
Here we were kindly met.
May the spotted cows thrive in this household,
May the horses grow strong and clear.[54]

And, as usual, there were predictions. It was said that the weather which prevailed at Mārtiņi would prevail at the winter solstice as well. Contrariwise, it was sometimes predicted that if it were freezing upon Mārtiņi, it would be warm around the solstice.

Magical Working

Needless to say, this is a superb time for a costume party with a great deal of dancing. Spanking may be considered optional.

Thirteen

Family Ceremonies

Ritual and ceremony were not limited to the eight festivals of the year which have been described in the previous chapters. It pervaded "ordinary" human life as well, and in a sense, it made "ordinary" existence extraordinary. Though family rites such as baptism and marriage retain some ritualistic elements in Catholicism and Eastern Orthodox Christianity, many Europeans and Euro-Americans lead lives devoid of ritual. This is especially true of Protestantism, which set out from its very inception to eradicate ritual from religion. (It also attempted to eradicate those who practiced such rituals in ordinary life. Though cultural myth enjoys blaming the witch trials on Catholic institutions such as the Inquisition, the fact is that the notorious Inquisitors had almost nothing to do with it, and witch persecution was relatively uncommon in the Catholic Mediterranean. Statistically speaking, the majority of "witches" were condemned not by Catholic ecclesiastical courts but by Protestant civil courts.)

It has been stated in the present volume earlier but is worth stating again: Paganism is less a "religion" than it is a way of life. Ritual activity plays a role in all aspects of human existence, and the goddesses and gods are with us always.

As an illustration, let us follow the life of a fictional village woman from medieval Lithuania, before Europe's last Pagan nation was officially "converted" in 1386. We shall call her Ona.

THE NAMING CEREMONY

Though her parents already knew that they intended to name the new baby Ona, they would not mention it to anyone until the *vardyny* or Naming Ceremony, for it was believed that practitioners of black magic could use people's names to gain power and control over them, or to bring illness to others, especially children. Therefore Ona's name would be kept secret.

In fact, Ona herself would be kept secret, hidden in the protection of her family home immediately after her birth, with her mother remaining in the house and receiving no visitors until after the new baby was formally—and ritualistically—introduced into the village community with the Naming Ceremony. Meanwhile, a tree would be planted near the farmstead gate and dedicated to the new child. Since the baby was a girl, Ona's parents planted a linden tree, sacred to Laima, the goddess who watched over all matters concerned with women.

As we have seen, Baltic Pagans believed in reincarnation, though the concept was not limited to incarnation as a human being but included all beings, all of whom were regarded as fully sentient. When a child was first born, the people believed that the child's soul was still in a kind of middle world between one lifetime and another. In a world where infant mortality was common, it was important to strengthen the child in their new life—and in fact, part of the Naming Ceremony would consist of separating Ona from her former life and fully inducting her into her new one.

When it was time for the Naming Ceremony, the participants would prepare themselves by washing. Ideally, they would undergo a complete cleansing in the sauna, though it would suffice simply to wash their hands and face with water from a jug if they did not have that opportunity. White garments were preferred, for white symbolized new beginnings, including the beginning of a new life.

Little Ona would be placed on a linen mat (note the symbolic white linen once again, so often mentioned in ceremonies involving the ancestors) or held in her mother's arms and swung back and forth while a song was sung. One of the participants would then wash Ona with water in a basin while the other participants lit candles to bless the child. They then threw money into the water basin as a kind of offering to the gods, though it would, in time, be collected by the woman who had performed the washing. A branch of rowan or juniper would be placed in the water and Ona would be smudged with one or another type of herb, most commonly rue.

Ona's hair—just one month's growth of it—would be cut as well. This symbolized cutting away her previous life so that she might grow into her new one. Her parents would bury her hair beneath the new linden tree they had planted to honor her arrival in the world and the community.

After having been washed and cleansed, Ona would be taken to the family's home altar or shrine, which was typically in or near the sauna. There, offerings would be made to some of the principal goddesses, especially Laima (Goddess of Women), Gabija (Guardian of the Hearth in the child's home), and Žemyna (Goddess of Childbirth, who would be thanked for Ona's healthy entry into this world). A ladle of beer or mead would be poured onto the ground. Bread would be offered. Linen towels would be left in the sauna, or, if the ceremony did not take place at the sauna, perhaps laid upon stones near a stream.

The participant who took on the role of washing Ona in the basin would now ask her parents if they were ready to accept a new guest into the family. The parents would, of course, answer yes, and then the special participant would ask what the new family member's name would be. It is at this point that her name, Ona, would first be spoken. After her name had been called, the father would tie a ribbon onto her to mark her entry into both family and community, and he would lift her into the air three times, after which Ona would be regarded as a full member of the community.

THE MAIDEN'S FAREWELL

And so, Ona grew up. Hers was a world of tasks on the family farm, enlivened by the annual festivals we have described in previous chapters, and by a fair amount of sexual experimentation with the village lads as well. Not all *dainas* and *dainos* deal with goddesses, gods, and religious festivals. Some are songs of love and passion—and some of those which are attributed to young women are lewd enough to drop more than a few jaws even in our modern society. There would be leaping over Midsummer fires and lusty forays into the woods to search for the fire-fern.

And yet, eventual marriage was always assumed, and that would change everything.

In ancient Greece, young women who were engaged to be married went to the temple of Aphrodite, and there they laid their most seductive garments, their most erotic perfumes, and their special combs and hair ornaments upon the altar of the Goddess of Love. And they left them there, for these were offerings to a goddess to whom they were now saying farewell. They were embarking upon a different kind of life, one that was sacred to Hera rather than to Aphrodite, and it would be Hera whom they worship from hereon.

For indeed, love and passion are about love and passion, and nothing else, but marriage was about contract, obligation, family responsibilities, and children.

The same philosophy prevailed upon the Pagan Amber Coast. As with any true initiation, there was a symbolic death and then a rebirth into a new way of life. Indeed, what we might call a "bachelorette party" wasn't much like one final exuberant blow-out. It was more like a funeral—suitable for a death and rebirth motif in the sense that Ona would be dying to love and romance, freedom and passion, and she would be saying hello to family life, complete with hard work, numerous responsibilities, children, and of course, a husband.

For Ona, it was very much like a funeral, for she had grown up not only pleasingly plump and pretty but good-natured as well, a favorite of the village boys. There was a great deal of joy for her to relinquish. But she had caught the eye of a fine young man named Gediminas, strong and hard-working, and in a position to inherit quite a prosperous farm.

Before Ona's friends gathered for the final celebration of her maidenly, unmarried years, she had to go around the village and make apologies to everyone in every house, in every shop—not only to the adults but even to the children. Several of her bridesmaids would accompany her on her journey. To each person, she would say something like: "Dear neighbor, please forgive me if I have ever offended you, or spoken bad words against you, or caused you harm, if merely by accident. And now, upon my final evening, I ask your blessing."

And by tradition, the blessing must be given. Here again, we see the funereal element: One way of life is ending, and a new way of life shall begin. It was a time of death and rebirth, and at such transitional moments, we are especially sensitive to any magic worked upon us by others, for all such magic is more likely to have a powerful effect as we hover between the worlds.

The party itself would be held at Ona's family home, the place where she grew up. This too was a kind of mourning, for she would be saying farewell to the only home she had ever known. Along the Amber Coast in Pagan days, the woman moved to the house of the husband at the time of marriage. Her girlhood home would be her home no more. When she returned from her apologetic circuit of the village, she would speak words such as: "There is no home like my father's home, no sycamore trees like its sycamore trees. It is rich with pearls and copper gates and silken curtains. Now open up the copper gate, my father, for your daughter enters, remembering the days of her youth and weeping."

Her father and mother would open the gate—a wooden one of course, not really shining copper—and Ona would speak words such as: "Thank you, my father, for raising me and for teaching me the skills of the world. No thanks, mother, for sending me to such a naughty boy, for ending my young days with their green roses."

MARRIAGE

The Pagan Balts celebrated weddings in a manner both cheerful and sad. There was dancing and music and joy, but a wedding was always tinged with sadness for the female side of life because the joys attendant upon life as a maiden were ending. The family home, the parents themselves, the young and still unmarried friends—all these things would become part of Ona's past now. A married woman no longer attended the parties held by her still unmarried friends, nor did she often dance at village festivals, for most of her time would now be devoted to household concerns and children.

Only married people were regarded as serious adults. Until then, they were unable to participate in community management or help solve important issues. Marriage gave a person a new status, and in that respect, it was a kind of initiation. And all initiations encompass both death and rebirth.

The wedding day itself would begin at dawn. The groom, Gediminas, and his party would dress in their finest clothes and begin to make their way to Ona's house.

Ona herself would already be in the midst of preparation. She must braid and comb her hair, and when she was finished, she had to throw the hairbrush into the household fire. The bridesmaids, who were sitting and standing at her side, did the same, singing songs to wish Ona a happy married life.

A wreath was woven for her by the eldest bridesmaid, and then she would dress for the wedding. However, Ona would not garb herself in the finest fashions of the day. Instead, she would dress in extremely old-fashioned clothes, as her ancestors would have dressed, for, after all, she was following in their footsteps, continuing the tradition.

After she was dressed, she would say farewell to her household gods, the spirits with whom she had lived since birth. Prayers had to be said to the principal goddesses of women's ways—Laima, Žemyna, and Gabija.

And then she must prepare herself to meet the groom.

Meanwhile, Gediminas and his party had reached the gate of Ona's family farm, only to encounter a team of bridesmaids guarding the entrance, tossing obstacles into their path, preventing them from entry unless they were able to answer a number of riddling questions. Typically, the groom himself would not answer. That task was up to an individual called "the suitor," roughly equivalent to what we call "the best man," or sometimes it was up to one of the groom's sisters.

Some of the kinds of questions and answers that were part of this repartee might have been as follows:

"Who are you?"

"Absent guests."

"Are there many of you here?"

"As many as the rays of the sun, as many as the grains of sand in the sea, as many as the leaves on the trees."

"And which path did you take?"

"A path made from the flowers of flax, bright with stars and sprinkled with green berries."

"What do you want here?"

"We want to stay the night and drink good beer and mead. We are weary, for we swam across the ocean and wandered through green forests."

In time, of course, the groom's party would be admitted. But by this time, some of the bridesmaids would have ritually hidden Ona beneath a large, specially prepared shirt. The best man would ask Ona's parents if his party may go and look for a goose—which, of course, meant Ona. The best man or "suitor" then approached the shirt and its guard of bridesmaids.

Once he had confronted the bridesmaids who held the shirt over Ona, he would say:

"I want to catch a goose. Which one will you give me?"

And the chief bridesmaid would reply: "Choose the one you like."

After a bit of playful scuffling, Ona would be brought out from beneath the shirt and taken to where all her relatives were waiting at the family shrine. The fire was lit at the shrine while prayers and offerings of salt were made to Gabija, Goddess of the Hearth Fire. Other goddesses and gods would most likely have been honored as well, especially Žemyna, who protects women and, in a sense, gives birth to all life on earth. Offerings to Žemyna typically included bread, which was buried in the ground (for Žemyna is the earth itself), and beer or mead would be passed around in a circle, with everyone pouring a bit on the ground before drinking and offering good wishes to one and all. Since it was assumed that the new bride, Ona, would someday have children, it would also be important to honor Laima, Goddess of Fate, for she was the patroness of women in childbirth as well as marriage and family. Bread and drink were typical offerings for Laima as well as for Žemyna. And in any important ceremony, Perkūnas should never be forgotten. In terms of weddings, he represented the male principle, and once again the beer or mead would be passed around.

A ceremonial ribbon would be blessed by passing it around the circle of guests, all of whom would touch it and send their positive energy into it mentally. Then the ribbon would be tied around the hands of Ona and her new husband, and hopes would be voiced that the two of them should never be untied until death. With their hands tied, Gediminas and Ona would be led around the altar three times, and the guests would shower them with grain as they circled the sacred fire. After their circuit around the altar was completed, their hands were untied, and the ribbon would be given to the young couple as the first sacred object of their marriage and the family which was expected to be born to them soon. Gediminas would wrap an expensive new cloak around Ona's shoulders and kiss her for the first time (or at least for the first time as her husband). The cloak symbolized care and protection. A drink would be brought to the newlyweds in a special wedding cup. They would drink from the cup with one ladle and feed each other honey.

The wreath would then be removed from Ona's head, and she would dance a dance in which she leapt in a circle with each of her bridesmaids, crowning each of them in turn with the wreath, and finally bestowing it upon her younger sister. The bridesmaids would then form a circle around the newlyweds and light candles to symbolize that their lives together should be filled with light. The parents of both Ona and Gediminas would serve them bread, salt, and beer.

Now the wedding feast could begin at a table in the garden, but first, the bride and groom would walk silently around the table in a circle, followed by the bridesmaids, then the groomsmen, then the rest of the guests. The table would be circled three times, and the parents of both partners gave their blessings to the newly married couple.

A gingerbread cake was then served, decorated with symbols of the World Tree, birds, and cows. An egg and a coin had been baked inside the cake.

After the meal, the dancing would begin. By tradition, the first dance would feature Gediminas partnering with Ona's sister and Ona with Gediminas' brother. Afterward, Ona and Gediminas would dance together. There would be leaping and jumping, as usual. Then, Ona and Gediminas would be led to the barn where they would sleep together for the first time as man and wife. In the morning, Ona would leave her home and go with Gediminas to his farm, where it was expected that she would spend the rest of her life.

Life in medieval Lithuania was much like life elsewhere in medieval Europe, with one important difference: Lithuania stubbornly remained Pagan.

Adjusting to married life was difficult for Ona at first. Always more of a lover than a worker, she was not particularly eager to share heavy farm chores with Gediminas' mother and sister. But Ona was not the type to enjoy being the laughingstock of the village, and so she soon began to shoulder her responsibilities with a bit more grace and proved to be an efficient worker, one who relied on her cleverness rather than her physical strength.

Her first child was a boy, born when she was nineteen, healthy from birth and a vigorous, active child. They named him Jurģi. That was, of course, a Christian name, and the feast of Úsiņi was already known to some as the feast of Jurģi, but the name seemed to suit him, and after all, a name was just a name. Then came a daughter. She was called Milda, after the Goddess of Love, and in time she would prove herself even closer in spirit to that benevolent goddess even than Ona. Several years later, another daughter arrived, and she was Ona's favorite. Sadly enough, she didn't last long in this world and passed away of a fever at the age of three. Laima and her sisters had cut the thread of the child's fate quite quickly. And while Ona continued to join the other village women whenever they gathered at the sauna to celebrate a new birth and offer their thanks to Laima, Ona never quite trusted the Goddess of Fate again. She sought the help of Perkūnas in protecting her children, and she carved or painted his sigil here and there all around the farm. She kept a *žaltys* snake behind the stove to honor Saulė and to protect the house. But of all the deities, her favorite was Gabija, for she loved to sit by the fire on cold winter nights.

Though Ona had her issues with the Goddess of Fate, she loved the linden tree by the gate which had been planted when she was born. It was *her* tree, after all. Despite the fact that the linden was Laima's sacred tree, Ona loved the tree itself. She often told family members that she hoped she would be reincarnated as a linden tree.

Time moved on, and Ona was widowed shortly before her fortieth year when Gediminas fell from his horse, broke his back, and never recovered. But Ona's son Jurġi was as clever as he was strong, and he was quick to take on control of the farm. To add to the bounty of the family, Ona's daughter would marry a wealthy merchant, though her flirtatious temperament proved to be a favorite topic of village gossip even after she became a wife.

Though Ona mourned for Gediminas, it cannot be said that her life was unpleasant. She would continue to live at the farm, and her son looked after her very well. She had always been kind and of a loving disposition; Ona had many friends. Though she didn't always trust Laima, the Goddess of Fate was kind to her and allowed her to keep her good looks even in her forties. She became even more plump than before; a robust physique was admired as a sign of good health, while women who were quite thin always seemed—at least in a world of farmers—to be somewhat unwell, and a bit too fragile for the vigorous life of the village. Ona always attended the summer solstice festivals crowned with a wreath of flowers every year. She became a favorite with the men of the village, and especially the young unmarried lads, for when asked if she would care for a romp in the woods—to seek the magic fire-fern, of course—she said yes more often than no.

And there were other occasions upon which Ona spent her time in the woods. Shortly after the turn of her fiftieth year, a rooster began to appear in the farmyard. He was an aggressive, blustery fellow with a colorful tail. Soon he became unafraid to strut into the house. He took up residence there, much to the chagrin of the house snake. Ona was convinced that he might be an aitvaras. Her son scoffed at the notion, but Ona would not let it go. She didn't want it to steal things from the neighbor's houses. May the gods forbid! Ona had always been on good terms with everyone in the village and wanted to stay that way.

But she really did want to see the aitvaras transform itself into a dragon. She had never seen a dragon, and neither had anyone else in the village.

Whenever the rooster wandered off into the woods beyond the farm, Ona followed him. She was convinced that if she followed him long enough, she would see him transform himself. It was said that an aitvaras would always become a dragon when outside of the house.

She had always been one to search for the magical fire-fern, and now she was off on another quest for magic. But her fire-fern expeditions had always been simply excuses to meet with lovers, as they were for everyone else. That was what her family believed she was doing now.

But they were wrong. This time Ona walked alone, following the rooster, hoping to see a real dragon. But the rooster always proved elusive, and Ona always ended up alone, sitting on a log, listening to the birds and pondering about life.

She became quieter and quieter, and in time her robust health would begin to fade. Each winter, she coughed harder and longer and spent more time sitting in silence by the fire, as if communing with her favorite goddess, Gabija. Her thick frame would grow thin, and she lay longer in bed. One winter, at fifty-four years of age, she simply could not stop coughing. She was difficult to rouse in the morning, even for food. And one morning, she failed to be roused altogether. Laima and her sisters had cut the thread of Ona's fate.

FUNERALS

The people of the village would keep the customary vigil over Ona's dead body, which would be laid out at a table in her home. They would have prayed to the goddesses and gods, sung songs, played the bagpipes, and lit candles near her feet. Surrounding her, the house would have been decorated with fir branches.

The linden tree that had been planted at her birth—the one she had always loved so much—would be cut down, and part of it would be used to fashion a *kankle,* a stringed instrument from the zither family, and the songs that marked her passing would be played upon it. The voice of the *kankle* was regarded as Ona's voice. Its sound was a kind of link between the worlds of the living and the dead, a connection to the spirits of the ancestors, a sign to her ancestors that it was time for them to accept her into their community. The village musicians would write lamentations in her honor, and they would be sung by the villagers who were of fine and lovely voice—though the singing would frequently be interrupted with weeping.

A table would be set up next to Ona's body. One of the older men in the village would brew beer, as was customary. When he was done, Ona's son Jurģi would roll the barrel out to the room where the mourners sat. The ritual question would then be asked: "Who is serving us this brew?" And the son would give the ritual answer: "Ona is serving you tonight." Then everyone would sit down for a feast. It was as if Ona herself were there, partaking of the meal, just as the ancestors came to eat with the living during the days of late autumn and winter.

And there would be laughter along with the lamentation. Jokes and amusing stories would be told. Laughter would make Ona's spirit feel happy and encourage her to pass through the gates of reincarnation and join her community again by returning in a new life.

Near the building where all the tools and working equipment of the farm were kept, a funeral pyre would be erected. In the morning, Ona would be cremated in the old-fashioned way rather than having her entire body buried in the ground, as some were now inclined to do, especially those influenced by the Christian folk.

After the burning of the body, the ashes would be placed in an urn and the urn crowned with a wreath—oak if the deceased was male, and if female…linden, of course.

A kind of altar would be constructed to be carried at the front of the funeral procession. It would be lit up with candles which would please Ona's spirit, for Gabija the Fire Goddess had always been her favorite. As the procession to the cemetery began, the mourners would have scattered grain upon the urn to wish Ona strength for her journey through the Otherworld to the realm of the ancestors, where a part of her would join the community of all those who came before, while another aspect of her soul continued journeying to reincarnate into a new life. A group of villagers who had learned the ancient songs closely followed the altar of fire, singing as they walked. Then came the urn itself, then the crowd of friends and other mourners.

When the cemetery was reached, the assembly would pause for a moment beside the grave. A few would make speeches; a hymn honoring all the ancestors would be sung. The village wise man or wise woman would say prayers to Žemyna and to Perkūnas as the *kankle* played on.

First, the fire on the altar would be extinguished and then lowered into the grave, followed by the urn itself. Those who had carried the altar, sung the songs, or played the music would each pour three handfuls of earth into the grave and chant, "May the Earth be easy upon you."

After the urn had been buried, it would be time to gather lunch. A place for Ona would be set as well. The village elder or perhaps Ona's closest friend—who in this case would be the woman who had acted as her principal bridesmaid so many years ago—would pour the beer or mead upon the ground, speaking a blessing to Žemynelė, the Earth God or masculine aspect of Žemyna, then turn to the empty place set for Ona at the table and say something in the manner of: "Beloved friend Ona, may the gods keep your spirit forever alive."

The best friend would then drink from the cup and hand it to another. The cup was passed around. Words of joy and gratitude for Ona and the life she had lived would be said. In time, the mourners would all go to their homes.

Ona's son and daughter would mourn her for an entire year. They would gather at special times on the third, sixth, ninth, and fortieth day after the funeral to speak of their mother and mention her name. On such days, it was said that the spirit of the deceased was present, listening as her name was called.

In time, it would be believed that she had truly passed. A part of her had become a member of the assemblage of the ancestors, who welcomed her through the gates of the dead. Now, Ona too could be called upon for help and healing, for aid and assistance to the living.

And another part of her soul would linger around the house, taking the sunlight and doing her business as always…Let us remember that the linden tree which marked her birth had been cut down at her death. In the spring, her son Jurģi discovered that a new linden tree was beginning to grow nearby, seeded, no doubt, from the old one. He honored it, and so did Ona's daughter Milda. During their own sojourn upon the earth, the Grand Duke Vytautas would make the pronouncement that Lithuania was now a Christian land. But, like most Lithuanians, Ona's son and daughter paid no heed to such political pronouncements. It was of no interest to them. They continued to praise and honor and, during festival times, to decorate her tree for the rest of their lives.

Ona's tree would be in blossom in the summer of 1410 when her grandson, named Gediminas after his grandfather, would join the Grand Duke Vytautas in the Lithuanian forces at the Battle of Grunwald.

Part V: The End of Pagan Europe

Fourteen

Pagan Europe's Last Stand: Grunwald, 1410

The Baltic was the last Pagan region in Europe. Even stubborn Scandinavia and distant Iceland had been converted to Christianity, even though most of the people continued to keep many of the old ways. There was a remote Christian outpost along the Amber Coast in what was then called Livonia, and which comprises modern-day Latvia and Estonia. It was at the mouth of the sacred Daugava (now Dvina) River. Founded in 1201, it is now present-day Riga, the capital of Latvia. As usual, mercantile and missionary interests were combined; merchants of the late medieval period involved in the fur trade found great riches in the Baltic, and the lonesome missionaries who lived there along with them worked hard at converting the populace, despite the fact that they were often killed and cut into pieces.

In 1202, the Christian community in Riga formed a military order similar to other orders of Crusader knights such as the Templars or Hospitallers. They were known as the "Brothers of the Sword." At first, they were successful in their battles against the Pagans, and Livonia was declared to be "officially" converted to Christianity in 1206.

Many Livonians, however, did not agree—especially the Estonians, who continued to rebel and fight against the Brothers of the Sword. In 1236, at the Battle of Saulė, the Estonians won such a decisive victory that, in essence, they wiped the Brothers of the Sword out almost completely.

Then, in the wake of the Sword Brothers' crushing defeat, the Teutonic Knights entered the scene.

The crusading Order of the Teutonic Knights was the nemesis of Baltic Paganism. Formed in Jerusalem around the same time as the other orders of knightly crusaders, the Teutonic Knights began returning to Europe as the Muslims persistently drove the Crusader Christian states and their inhabitants out of the Near East. For a time, the Teutonic Knights were employed by the King of Hungary to fight against steppe nomads who threatened his kingdom. But it soon became apparent that the Knights had more on their minds than defending a Christian nation; their true passion was real estate rather than religion. In 1225, after they had driven out the people they'd been hired to protect and snatched up the rights to their lands, the Hungarians told them to move along and practice their acquisitive habits elsewhere.

They turned their attention to the Pagans of the Amber Coast.

Christian Poland fought constantly with Pagan Prussia to the northeast; its efforts were unsuccessful and frustrating. Then, the Teutonic Knights arrived. Armed with the express permission of the Holy Roman Emperor to Christianize the Prussians by force, if necessary, the Teutonic Knights and Poland allied with each other to launch an invasion of Prussia in 1230. As with the Hungarians before them, it was an alliance that the Poles would learn to regret.

The Teutonic Knights fought their way into Prussia with great difficulty. They may have been well-trained in military matters, but the Prussian warriors were fierce and dedicated, and not in the mood to surrender their homeland. They fought, from one village to the next, for years. The carnage was great on both sides. Nevertheless, when the Brothers of the Sword were destroyed at the Battle of Saulė in 1236, the Teutonic Knights found enough time and manpower to send some of their own members to Riga, where they became known as the *Livonian Order* and took up the struggle against Baltic Paganism in the north. And, as usual, they pushed things a bit too far in their eternal quest for new real estate to acquire. In an attempt to invade Russia, they were defeated by Alexander Nevsky of Novgorod at the Battle of the Ice in 1242, an event which was memorably depicted in the 1938 film *Alexander Nevsky* by the legendary Sergei Eisenstein.

For the most part, however, the Teutonic Knights prevailed, both in Livonia against the still rebellious Estonians, and, very slowly, against the Prussians farther south. By 1290, Estonian resistance had been crushed. Meanwhile, the Prussians were displaced from their lands as soon as a new region was conquered; the Knights invited colonists from Holland, Flanders, Poland, and of course, Germany to occupy the newly won lands. In time, the few remaining Prussians were assimilated into a culture which was primarily German in nature, and their language, now known as "Old Prussian" and cited at various times in this book, became extinct.

The Teutonic Knights had done what the Poles had asked them to do; they had conquered the Prussians. But Poland had rather expected that some of the lands won by the Knights would become part of Poland. The Knights made it clear that this was not to be the case. As usual, real estate rather than religion was foremost on their minds, and they created their own state in what had once been Prussia. They began to treat the Poles like enemies, and Poland was sorry it had ever invited these marauders into their borders.

In time, Lithuania remained alone as the last Pagan nation in Europe. And though it was surrounded by the Teutonic Knights both to the north and the south, the Grand Duchy of Lithuania continued to grow and become powerful until the last Pagan state in Europe was also the largest European polity, comprising not only modern Lithuania but present-day Belarus and Ukraine as well as parts of Poland and Russia. Pagan Lithuania included a large number of Catholics and Eastern Orthodox Christians and was renowned for its policy of religious tolerance, a statement which could not be made regarding any of the surrounding Christian countries. Though the Teutonic Knights had waged campaigns against Lithuania in the 1200s, the Grand Duchy had grown so enormous by the middle 1300s that even the battle-hungry Knights were reluctant to attack it.

Lithuania became nominally Catholic in 1386, but this was a matter of political expediency rather than religious fervor. Jogaila, the Grand Duke of Lithuania, aspired to marry Jadwiga of Poland, but the young lady was passionately Christian and refused to marry a Pagan. Jogaila converted to Christianity, became the King of Poland under the name of Władysław II Jagiełło, and his cousin

Vytautas ruled as Grand Duke of Lithuania, achieving a number of conquests which stretched the borders of Lithuania to their greatest extent. Despite his official "conversion" to Christianity in 1386 to keep his cousin Jogaila firmly in control of Poland, Vytautas made no attempt to impose Christianity on the still-Pagan population of Lithuania, and churchmen accused him of going to a Catholic church on Sundays while continuing to celebrate the ancient Pagan holidays. The Teutonic Knights complained that both Jogaila and Vytautas had converted only for political gain and that both of them were still secretly Pagan. The Knights were most likely correct in the case of Vytautas, though Jogaila's Christianity appears to have been genuine.

Jadwiga died young during childbirth in 1399, leaving the Lithuanian Jogaila as King of Poland. He was a dour fellow, lean and of stooped posture, thin-lipped and seldom loquacious. He loved hunting and frequently retreated on long hunts that gave him the opportunity to ponder his political strategies. Vytautas was quite different; a natural warrior, he was big and blustery and well-liked for his effusive personality. But there was one thing the two rulers, so different in character, could agree upon: territorial disputes with the military/religious state of the Teutonic Knights who were wedged in between them had reached the point where there could be no more agreement.

In 1410, Jogaila and Vytautas joined forces to do battle with the Knights. The conflict would take place in Prussia, on territory occupied by the Teutonic Knights. Vytautas led his Pagan army from Lithuania into the kingdom of Poland to rendezvous with Jogaila's army and confront the Teutonic Knights. His forces were made up of a hodge-podge of Lithuanians, Russians, and even Tartars from the Central Asian steppes with whom Vytautas had made both war and peace in Russia over the years. Jogaila, ever the strategic thinker, made sure all the river crossings along the route were well guarded so that the Knights couldn't prevent Vytautas from crossing the rivers and arriving for battle in time. The Lithuanians made their way through dense forests which many would have regarded as impassable, but some of Vytautas' men were veterans who had fought in rough country during the Russian campaigns, and the Tartars among them made excellent scouts.

While the combined armies of Poland and Lithuania outnumbered the Knights, many of them were undisciplined and inexperienced. Ona's grandson Gediminas, for example, had never wielded anything more deadly than a farm tool in his life. The Teutonic Knights, while lesser in number, were professional fighting machines. In those days, the leaders, even if they were kings, typically rode into battle in the front lines along with their men, but Jogaila and Vytautas were both about sixty years of age, Jogaila was in poor health and commanded strategically from the rear, while it was Vytautas, ruler of Europe's last Pagan nation, who would lead the troops into battle against the Christian crusaders.

At first, the two armies faced each other across a river; but then it seemed as if Jogaila and the Poles were retreating. Ulrich of Jungingen, the grandmaster of the Teutonic Knights, rushed through the woods to cut off their retreat. His men marched all night, only to find themselves facing the Poles and Lithuanians early the next morning. Both forces lined up; then they waited. Jogaila sat in his tent on top of a hill and seemed disinclined to begin the conflict. Meanwhile, the heavily armored Knights stood for several hours in the blazing sun of July 15 until they were tired, weary, and discouraged—which was precisely the way Vytautas wanted them to be.

At last, the rival armies charged at each other and engaged in full combat. Vytautas led a combined force of Lithuanians and Poles straight into the Teutonic Order's midst, while farther down the line, another force of Lithuanians and Tartars appeared to retreat. Overjoyed, the Knights pursued them. Soon, they found themselves in a deep forest, and the Pagan Lithuanians—who had in fact only pretended to retreat in order to draw the Knights into the woods—re-emerged from the forest like spirits of Nature and began slaughtering the Knights.

When word reached the grandmaster of the disaster in the woods, and as Vytautas pressed harder and harder into the center of the Order's forces, Jungingen realized that he could not retreat. Behind him was yet another deep stand of forest—if his men tried to cut their way through it, the pursuing Lithuanians would easily catch up with them and slaughter them. The grandmaster did the only thing he could do. He ordered his men to charge, and he headed straight for the hill where he believed the Polish king was waiting.

But Jogaila wasn't there. In another one of his strategic moves, he had disappeared to a more remote location. But he was recognized, and the Germans headed for him. If they could bring down Jogaila, they would win the battle. Quickly assessing the situation, Vytautas rode at top speed to Jogaila and urged him to commit his reserve unit to battle. Jogaila took the Grand Duke's advice; his personal reserves charged the Knights. The battle became a slaughter. Jungingen, the grandmaster of the Teutonic Knights, was slain on the field, and his forces fled back to the wagon camp, followed not only by Jogaila's personal forces and Vytautas' Pagan warriors but by the other band of Lithuanians who had staged the mock retreat into the forest and who now came to rejoin the battle.

At the wagon camp, chaos ensued. Jogaila's personal forces were equally engaged in killing Germans and in raiding the wine casks that were stored at the wagon camp—in the latter objective, they were aided by the "camp followers" (a euphemism for "prostitutes"[55]) who enjoyed the wine just as much as the troops did. Jogaila—himself a non-drinker in an age of heavy drinking—had to put in a personal appearance and order his men to stop raiding the wine casks, for he was well aware of what the combination of too much wine and boiling hot weather could do.[56]

At this point, the battle was effectively over. The power that the Teutonic Knights had wielded over Eastern Europe for two hundred years was broken, the grandmaster killed, and the majority of the active fighting force slain upon the battlefield. The triumph of Poland and Lithuania was complete. No more would the Knights torment and murder those who still professed a Pagan faith.

And yet, as the old saying goes: "They won the battle, but they lost the war."

The warriors who returned in triumph from the Battle of Grunwald were returning to a world which was already in the midst of change. The Old Prussians, who to many had been a familiar population of Baltic Pagans, were virtually gone, destroyed, assimilated into a different—and thoroughly Christian—culture. In Livonia, the Latvians were beginning to take Christianity seriously; we have already seen how the names and the timing of the major festivals were changed to fit in with the feast days of various saints. That process, perhaps, was already beginning. Even the rebellious Estonians were beginning to accept their new status as Christians.

Vytautas of Lithuania, the victor at the Battle of Grunwald, continued to practice religious tolerance. He ruled over an empire which included Pagans, Eastern Orthodox Christians, Catholics, and Muslims, and he made no effort to force any of his subjects into a different religion—a truly unusual stance for a medieval ruler to take. Lithuanians still refer to him as Vytautas the Great, and modern Lithuania's principal university is named for him.

But if Vytautas practiced absolute tolerance, not all his successors did the same. There were many who supported the efforts of Catholic missionaries to Christianize the country folk of Lithuania. In general, the missionaries were somewhat less than successful, though certain customs faded over the next several hundred years—the *žaltys* snakes were no longer welcome to live behind the stove, and the sacred serpents passed out of the house and into folklore. In Lithuania, probably the most stubbornly Pagan of all the peoples of the Amber Coast, things changed slowly. It is sometimes said that the rural population remained essentially Pagan until the middle 1700s. Nevertheless, the world had changed, and things were no longer as they used to be.

Young Gediminas noticed it even on his way home from the battle. For a time, he rode with other warriors who were traveling in the same direction, but for the last few days before reaching home, he rode alone. He noticed that there were more wooden crosses topping the roofs of farmhouses than there had been when he was a boy. He stopped and asked for shelter one night, and the farmer's wife kept both a cross on the stove and a snake behind it—there was no point in not covering all one's bases. In the morning, the sun was bright and he noticed the beauty of the roses that bloomed in front of the house. His hostess was kind enough to give him some seeds.

When he reached his home, his father Jurģi was tending the barley fields as usual, and his mother was cooking. His aunt Milda was lending a hand—apparently, she was staying away from the village center after having played the leading role in the latest summer solstice scandal. A neighbor by the bane of Inija was helping to stir the pot as well—though young, she was the best cook of the three and Gediminas had often thought she might make quite a good wife.

He would have to have a talk with her this evening, and perhaps they might take a walk in the twilight down by the river.

But there was something he had to do first.

He walked out to the farmyard gate, where the new linden tree was growing, robust and strong. He dug a hole near the base of the tree, and he planted the rose seeds that the farmwife with both the snake and the cross had given him.

This was the right place for them.

Ona had always loved roses.

The centuries passed, but a kernel of memory, sweet and tasty, remained within the Baltic peoples.

Fifteen

The Last Goddess

Euhemerism... Now there's a word which does not rest easily upon the tongue. It's a big word, and one which must be defined, for it is also a rather big concept. Let us call it our "word of the day."

Euhemerism is an idea named for its inventor, the Greek philosopher (and a writer of fiction, which may be a more important factor than his philosophy) Euhemerus, who probably lived in the fourth century BCE, although even this much is uncertain. His major work, entitled *Sacred History,* introduced the concept that the gods had originally been mortal human beings, but they came to be worshiped as deities because their achievements were so remarkable as to stand the test of time, and even to grow larger and more fabulous as the centuries moved on. Some early Christian writers deeply appreciated his work because it gave them a handy explanation that explained the reverence still given to Zeus, Dionysus, Aphrodite, and all the others during an era in which the early Church Fathers were trying to convince the Mediterranean world that there was only one god, and his name was Jesus. The others were simply mortals who, due to their outstanding deeds and qualities, had come to be worshiped over time. Euhemerus was eminently quotable in that respect. He explained it all.

Euhemerism later became exceptionally valuable to Norse writers as well, especially Snorri Sturluson (1179–1241), whose work, variously called the *Prose Edda* or *Younger Edda*, is one of our most important sources of Viking mythology. But Snorri was a Christian, and though his literary affection for the old goddesses and gods of Norse lore is quite obvious in his writing, he could not worship them. Euhemerism proved to be a useful tool for Snorri; he wrote that Odin was a king and warlord who had migrated with his people from the steppes of Central Asia to what is now Scandinavia and later became worshiped as a god. Thor, Freyr, and Freya could be explained in similar fashion.

Though euhemerism was a blessing to medieval Christian writers in search of a logical explanation for Pagan deities, it is universally rejected by all modern scholars.

Euhemerism is simply a cultural fallacy, a ragged left-over from Classical Greece with no relevance at all to the contemporary study of Pagan myth.

In Chapter Six, which chronicled the legend of Jūratė and Kastytis, we paid a brief visit to the town of Palanga, Lithuania's best-known beachside resort. Palanga commands attention for a number of reasons. Birutė Hill is the highest dune at Palanga and now a part of the Palanga Botanical Garden. Archaeological research indicates that there was a village at the bottom of the hill in the tenth century. Later, in the thirteenth century, the Teutonic Knights and their allied crusaders, the Livonian Order, invaded Palanga. The villagers built a defense system with a tower. After a defeat from which the Pagan population eventually recovered, the defense system was rebuilt and made even stronger; it now had two towers and a wall that surrounded the top of the hill.

In time, however, the Christian armies overwhelmed Palanga, and in 1506 the top of the eminence which is now called Birutė Hill was crowned with a chapel to St. George. In 1869 the chapel was rebuilt, and its current incarnation is now a popular tourist destination.

In 1989, a team of archaeologists, digging beneath the foundations of the Chapel of St. George, discovered a complex previously unknown, one which had somehow slipped away from the historical record—a Pagan sanctuary and astronomical observatory which dated from the late 1300s or early 1400s. This, of course, was after Lithuania's "official" conversion to Christianity in 1386. In fact, it appeared as if the Chapel of St. George had been erected over the

Pagan sanctuary in order to prevent people from practicing Pagan worship there.

The sanctuary and observatory were dedicated to a goddess called Birutė, who was widely reverenced by the people of Palanga and the region which surrounded it.

Birutė, however, was not a figure of Neolithic or Indo-European myth but a mortal woman, in fact, the mother of the legendary Vytautas the Great. She was born sometime around 1330 and died in 1382. In the fifteenth century, she was being worshiped as a goddess, though her precise function as a goddess is unknown. A chapel to St. George was built over her shrine, and St. George, as we have seen when we examined the Feast of Úsiņi in Chapter Ten, was a God of Nature whose festival was celebrated in the spring, so she may have been worshiped as a Goddess of Nature since this would allow local people to continue making the same offerings as always, offerings for good health and prosperity, which were the customary gifts bestowed upon mortals by goddesses and gods of Nature. But now the people must make those offerings in a new place, a Christian church. part of Birutė's former temple complex.

Here again is our "word for the day." Euhemerism.

Birutė was born about 1330, in a place unknown and to a family unknown, though her heritage must have been aristocratic since she attracted the attention of Kęstutis, the Grand Duke of Lithuania. She had chosen a religious rather than a conventional life and was a Pagan priestess serving one of the temples of the sacred fire as a perpetual celibate (rather like the priestesses described as guardians of the Tree of Romuva in Chapter One). Kęstutis heard rumors of her phenomenal beauty and paid a visit to the shrine just to meet her. He was immediately infatuated with her and begged her to marry him. She refused, preferring the virginal life of a Pagan priestess. Kęstutis acted upon his royal prerogative and, somewhere around 1349, he abducted her from the temple and married her against her will.

In time, Birutė settled into her new role as the Grand Duchess of Lithuania, bearing no less than six children to Kęstutis, including her first-born, the boy who grew up to be Vytautas the Great, the final defender of the Pagan faith which his mother had served as a priestess.

There is a certain mystery surrounding Birutė's death. Between 1381 and 1382 Kęstutis was involved in a number of political machinations which would end with Jogaila's marriage to Jadwiga and his accession as King of Poland, while Birutė's son Vytautas would in time become the Grand Duke of Lithuania. In the course of the squabbles, Kęstutis—who had remained stubbornly Pagan in an era when Lithuanian nobles were quickly converting to Christianity purely for the sake of political expediency—was captured and imprisoned by his old enemies the Teutonic Knights, and died during his imprisonment, whether by murder or from old age is unclear.

Birutė was also arrested by the Teutonic Knights and, allegedly "for her own safety" during Lithuania's internecine wars, was transported to the city of Brest in what is now Belarus. What happened to her there is unclear. Some say that she was drowned—perhaps assassinated—in a lake near Brest. This was firmly denied in 1407 at the Council of Constance. Other stories assert that she was eventually released, and that since she was a widow, she was able to return freely to her first love—acting as a Pagan priestess at the same shrine in Palanga where she had first chosen that path of life. In any event, she appears to have died in the year 1382, several years before her son Vytautas made yet another—and equally politically motivated—conversion to Christianity and ended Lithuania's status as the last Pagan nation in Europe.

The Stars of the Baltic

Lithuanian country folk believed that every person has a star. There was a saying: "There are as many stars in the sky as there are people on the earth." When a baby is born, its star lights up in the sky. The stars had the function of guardian angels. When a person is alive, the star guards and keeps the spirit in the body, and after death, the star lights up the path for the soul to journey to its place in the Otherworld.

A few names of important stars have been preserved, such as "The Maiden" (Capella) and "The Goat of Perkūnas" (Polaris), as well as the names of a number of constellations:

The Pleiades: The Sieve, The Sowers, or The Plovers

The Big Dipper: God's Horses or The Wagon of Perkūnas. (In other European societies, the Dipper was known as "King Arthur's Wagon" or "Charlemagne's Wagon.")

Corona Borealis: This seems to have been an important constellation in the Baltic, as it was to the Greeks and Celts since we have several names for it: The Flower Garden, The Lilac Garden, or The Garden of Paradise.

Orion: The Haymakers

Orion's Belt: The Three Sisters

The Milky Way: The Road of Souls or the Path of the Cranes (For more on the Milky Way as a pathway of the ancestors, see the section entitled "The Old Prussian Zodiac" in Chapter Eight. It is also probable that some references to the Daugava River refer to the Milky Way rather than the geographical river of that name. See the section on "The Sun Goddess" in Chapter Two.)

The presence of an astronomical observatory at Birutė's shrine suggests that she may have been considered to be a goddess of celestial matters rather than a Nature Goddess. Her observatory is worth a closer look.

The Palanga observatory is a horseshoe-shaped embankment which consisted of eleven wooden posts, most of them arranged in pairs. These posts marked important azimuths of the sun and moon. An azimuth is the angle between true north, measured clockwise from the observer's horizon, and a celestial body. It determines the direction of the celestial body. For example, a celestial body at due north has an azimuth of 0°, one at due east 90°, one due south 180° and one due west 270°. The poles at Birutė's observatory were oriented due west and hence marked the setting of the sun and moon into the Baltic Sea nearby. They also marked the two solstice points as well as the Metonic cycle, a nineteen-year cycle which may have allowed for the prediction of eclipses.

The stars and planets were observed by special prophets (men and women) called *žvaigždininkas* (a star man) or *krivis* (a priest). The observations were used to construct the calendar, to foresee important astronomical events, and to appoint the time for sacrificial rites. Crusader chronicles mention Prussian prophets called *tullissones* and *ligaschones* who took part in burial ceremonies and observed (apparently through mystical vision) the riding of souls on horseback across "the middle of the sky."

The Last Goddess may well have been the Goddess of the Sky.

When the Soviet Empire fell in 1989, it was the people of the Amber Coast who were the first to re-emerge with Neopagan organizations and reclaim the ancient heritage which stretched back, through the vastness of history and long before written language, into the earliest Indo-European times, and even into the distant reaches of the Neolithic.

Today, the Neopagan community thrives along the Amber Coast.

If you rise early, while the sun is at its 90° azimuth, and stride forth to work in your garden, I hope that you will remember the second and third chapters of this book, and if you are approached by elderly men or attractive women in unfashionable back-country clothes who render good advice about your garden, I hope that you will treat them kindly.

They just might be goddesses and gods.

Appendix

The Baltic Sigils and How to Use Them

During Pagan times, the people of the Amber Coast used the sigils of the Goddesses and Gods to invoke the gifts of that particular deity into their lives. Sigils were sometimes carved in wood, usually on the doors of houses or barns. Sometimes they were painted on doors and walls.

The World Tree: Protection of the family. Connects you with Dievas, gives strength and advice. Guardian of home and hearth.

GODDESSES AND GODS

Dievas: The dome of the sky; the universe. The protection of Heaven.

Perkūnas: Cross of Thunder. Solar energy. Protection of home and family.

Saulė: Sigil of the Sun and the World, this sigil also protects home and family.

Rosette of Saulė at Mid-Day: Popular for weddings and another family protector.

Aušrinė: Love and Beauty.

Māra: Creation and Birth.

Žemyna: Fertility of the Earth

Laima: Provides creativity and sensitivity, promotes love for elders, family members, and neighbors.

Jumis: Fruitfulness and blessings. Prosperity in the home.

Úsiņš: Creates light and protects against diseases.

THE FESTIVALS

Winter Solstice: Rebirth of the light, triumph of light over darkness, old age.

Meteņi: The beginning of spring, casting away the past.

The Vernal Equinox: Fertility, happiness, childhood.

Úsiņi: A celebration for our animals, the beginning of the summer.

The Summer Solstice: Youth, light, sex, joy.

Māras: Family, home, prosperity, the beginning of autumn.

The Autumn Equinox: Maturity, wealth, abundance.

Mārtiņi: The time of the ancestors, the beginning of winter.

Endnotes

PART I. THE WORLD TREE

Introduction

1 By "witches," one means herbalists and other folk healers who preferred to live in the forest where they could communicate with sacred trees, which were regarded as wisdom teachers—though these individuals were feared by the more settled villagers.

2 *The Odyssey*, cited by Marija Gimbutas in *The Balts*, New York, Praeger, 1963, p. 56.

3 Gimbutas, *ibid.*, p. 156.

4 Gimbutas, Marija. *The Goddesses and Gods of Old Europe: 6500–3500 BC, Myths and Cult Images* (Berkeley and Los Angeles: University of California Press, 1982); *The Language of the Goddess* (San Francisco: Harper and Row, 1989); and *The Civilization of the Goddess: The World of Old Europe* (San Francisco: Harper and Row, 1991).

5 Anthony, David. *The Horse, the Wheel, and Language*, Princeton, NJ, Princeton University Press, 2010, *passim.*

6 Stone, Merlin. *When God Was a Woman*, Boston, Houghton Mifflin, 1978, and Eisler, Riane. *The Chalice and the Blade*, Boston, Harper Collins, 1988.

7 For a non-academic summary of Gimbutas' change of opinion, see her preface to Metzner, Ralph *Well of Remembrance*, Boulder, CO, Shambhala, 2001, pp. xi-xii.

Chapter One: The Tree at the Heart of the World

8 Daina 34039-6, "The Song Cabinet," *dainuskapis.lv/katalogs*, accessed Nov 1, 2022.

9 This custom still survives in Eastern Europe. I have seen it practiced as recently as 1994–5.

10 Gimbutas. *The Balts, op. cit.*, p. 191.

PART II: GODDESSES AND GODS

Chapter Two: Heaven

11 Daina Ltdz III, 7718, *http://dievturi.blogspot.com/p/dievturiba.html,* retrieved Nov 10, 2022.

12 Daina 33671–2, "The Song Cabinet," *dainuskapis.lv/katalogs*, retrieved Nov 6, 2022.

13 Daina 33682-6, *ibid.*

14 Daina 33684-0, *ibid.*

15 Daina 66335-0, *ibid.*

16 Daina 33698-0, *ibid.*

17 In general, we shall use the Lithuanian form of her name, *Saulė,* which is more commonly known among folklore scholars, however; most of the *dainas* come from Latvia, and therefore our direct quotes from the old folk songs will spell her name as *Saulė,* the Latvian form of her name.

18 This poem is a mixture of several traditional dainas, and the arrangement is my own.

19 Daina 33821-0, *ibid.*

20 Daina 33820-0, *ibid.*

21 Daina 33827-3, *ibid.*

22 Daina 33827-9, *ibid.*

23 Daina 33788-3, *ibid.*

24 Daina 33829-2, *ibid.*

25 Daina 33738-4, *ibid.*

26 This poem is a mixture of several traditional dainas, and the arrangement is my own.

27 Daina 33813-0, *ibid.*

28 This poem is a mixture of several traditional dainas, and the arrangement is my own.

Chapter Three: Earth

29 *https://pruskiwicher.wordpress.com/bogowie-i-boginie/zemmina/* retrieved Nov 18.

30 Greimas, Algirdas. *Of Gods and Men*, Bloomington, IN, Indiana University Press, 1992, *passim.*

31 Daina LD 1176, *http://dievturi.blogspot.com/p/dievturiba.html,* retrieved Nov 10, 2022.

32 *Ibid.*

33 *https://pruskiwicher.wordpress.com/bogowie-i-boginie/laima/,* Retrieved Nov 13, 2022.

Chapter Four: The Underworld

34 The *dainos* quoted here are adapted from *http://romuva.lt/pas-auleziura/giesmes/giesmes-mildai/,* retrieved August 19, 2023.

35 Abbey, Edward. *The Journey Home: Some Words in Defense of the American West*, New York, Plume, 1991.

36 *https://pruskiwicher.wordpress.com/bogowie-i-boginie/ragana3/,* retrieved Nov 21.

PART III. LOVERS AND HEROES

Chapter Seven: Eglė, the Queen of Serpents

37 Campbell, Joseph. *The Masks of God.* Penguin Group, 1959.

38 Ginzburg, Carlo. *Ecstasies: Deciphering the Witches' Sabbath*, New York, Pantheon, 1991, *passim.*

Chapter Eight: The Baltic Calendar

39 For a typical example, see *http://dievturi.blogspot.com/p/dievturiba.html,* retrieved November 23, 2022.

40 *https://pruskiwicher.wordpress.com/pruski-kalendarz/,* retrieved November 23, 2022.

41 *Ibid.*

Chapter Nine: The Winter Festivals

42 "The Profane Art of Masking." *People of Goda, Clan of Tubal Cain*, http://www.clanoftubalcain.org.uk/masks.html.

43 Daina Ldz 13980 *http://dievturi.blogspot.com/p/dievturiba.html*, retrieved Nov 10, 2022.

44 *http://www.clanoftubalcain.org.uk/masks.html*, retrieved August, 2023

45 *https://pruskiwicher.wordpress.com/pruski-kalendarz/*, retrieved November 23, 2022.

Chapter Ten: The Springtime Festivals

46 Daina LTdz 14430 *http://dievturi.blogspot.com/p/dievturiba.html*, retrieved Nov 10, 2022.

47 *https://pruskiwicher.wordpress.com/bogowie-i-boginie/pergrubris/*, retrieved November 23, 2022

48 Daina LTdz 14579, *http://dievturi.blogspot.com/p/dievturiba.html*, retrieved Nov 10, 2022.

Chapter Eleven: The Summer Festivals

49 Alder and aspen were not always regarded as inauspicious trees. They had their times, their uses, and their special purposes—but not for the summer solstice festival.

50 Daina LTdz 16974, *http://dievturi.blogspot.com/p/dievturiba.html*, retrieved Nov 10, 2022.

51 This is a combination of several *dainas* as well as a few lines from other *dainas*, arranged by the present author.

52 Daina LTdz 16960, *http://dievturi.blogspot.com/p/dievturiba.html*, retrieved Nov 10, 2022.

Chapter Twelve: The Autumn Festivals

53 Daina 54316-16, "The Song Cabinet," *dainuskapis.lv/katalogs*, retrieved Nov 6, 2022.

54 Daina LTdz 14221, *http://dievturi.blogspot.com/p/dievturiba.html*, retrieved Nov 10, 2022.

Chapter Fourteen: Pagan Europe's Last Stand: Grunwald, 1410

55 The word "prostitute," though not used today, is the appropriate term for use in the thirteenth century.

56 Urban, William, *The Last Years of the Teutonic Knights: Lithuania, Poland, and the Teutonic Order*, London, Greenhill Books, pp. 164–198.

Bibliography

Abbey, Edward. *The Journey Home: Some Words in Defense of the American West*. Plume, 1991.

Anthony, David W. *The Horse, the Wheel, and Language*. Princeton University Press, 2010.

Campbell, Joseph. *The Masks of God*. Penguin Group, 1959.

Eisler, Riane. *The Chalice and the Blade*. Harper Collins, 1988.

Gimbutas, Marija. *The Balts*. Praeger, 1963.

—. *The Civilization of the Goddess*. Harper and Row, 1991.

—. *The Goddesses and Gods of Old Europe*. University of California Press, 1982.

—. *The Language of the Goddess*. Harper and Row, 1989.

Greimas, Algirdas J. *Of Gods and Men*. Indiana University Press, 1992.

Graves, Robert. *The White Goddess*. Farrar, Straus and Giroux, 1966.

Grunau, Simon. *Preussische Chronik*. 1517-1529.

Johnson, Kenneth. *Witchcraft and the Shamanic Journey*. Crossed Crow Books, 2022.

"Katalogs: Dainu Skapis. Latvju Dainas, Tautasdziesmas, Dziesmas." *Dainas: Dainu Skapis. Latvju Dainas, Tautasdziesmas, Dziesmas*, http://dainuskapis.lv/katalogs. Accessed Nov. 2022.

"Latvijas Dievturu Sadraudze: Dievturība." *Latvijas Dievturu Sadraudze*, http://dievturi.blogspot.com/p/dievturiba.html. Accessed Nov. 2022.

Metzner, Ralph. *Well of Remembrance*. Shambhala, 2001.

"Romuva: Romuva—Tai Senovės Baltų Religinė Bendrija." *Romuva*, http://romuva.lt. Accessed Nov. 2022.

"Pruski Wicher." *Pruski Wicher*, 7 Mar. 2013, https://pruskiwicher.wordpress.com/bogowie-i-boginie/zemmina/.

Stone, Merlin. *When God Was a Woman*. Houghton Mifflin Harcourt, 1978.

"The Profane Art of Masking." *People of Goda, Clan of Tubal Cain*, http://www.clanoftubalcain.org.uk/masks.html.

Urban, William. *The Last Years of the Teutonic Knights*. Greenhill Books, 2018.Stone, Merlin. *When God Was a Woman*. Houghton Mifflin Harcourt, 1978.

Urban, William. *The Last Years of the Teutonic Knights*. Greenhill Books, 2018.

INDEX

A

D

E

F

G

H

I

R

S

T

U

V

W

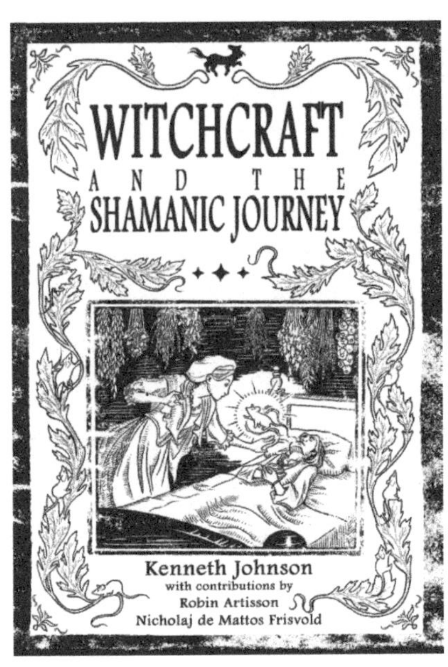

Witchcraft and the Shamanic Journey

KENNETH JOHNSON

This beautifully written book will show seekers of the magical arts how to reclaim the old traditions of our pagan ancestors, which, as this book will show, were heavily rooted in shamanism. Kenneth Johnson takes the reader on a journey far into the past where these shamanistic practices of medieval and Renaissance European people can be explored while simultaneously teaching the working Witch how to incorporate these older traditions into their own magical practice. Included in this book are explorations of the mystical otherworld, instructions on how to discover one's Tree of Power, methods of entering the World Mountain to gain wisdom, an in-depth overview of folkloric initiatory practices, the folklore of the Wild Hunt, and much more.

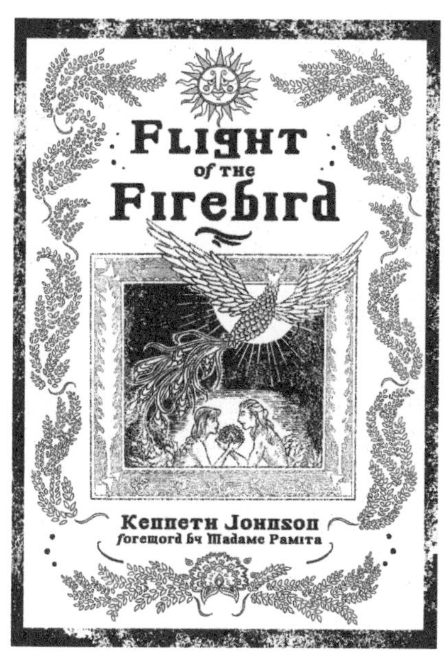

Flight of the Firebird

Slavic Magical Wisdom & Lore

KENNETH JOHNSON

Flight of the Firebird: Slavic Magical Wisdom & Lore by Kenneth Johnson is an incredible guide into the folk magical traditions of the Slavic peoples. Documenting his time spent studying with the magical practitioners abroad, Flight of the Firebird offers a unique perspective into the magical practices of an incredibly beautiful culture. The book is filled with the author's real-world experiences alongside the wisdom and teachings of the Slavic magical elders to create a highly engaging and quite operative book of magic and folklore.